A Primer for Local Historical Societies

A Primer for Local Historical Societies

by Dorothy Weyer Creigh

American Association for State and Local History

Nashville

Library of Congress Cataloging in Publication Data
Creigh, Dorothy Weyer.
  A primer for local historical societies.
  Bibliography: p.
  Includes index.
  1. Historical societies—United States. I. American
Association for State and Local History. II. Title.
E172.C783   973'.06'2   76–231
ISBN 0–910050–20–1

1400 Eighth Avenue, South
Nashville, Tennessee 37203

Printed in the United States of America

To the Adams County Historical Society

Lorraine, Charles, the two Bills, the two Larrys, Marie, Ellen, Thelma, Cathy, Lu, and all the others of us who have labored together through the years

May our work in the years to come be as challenging and as satisfying as it has been the past ten years.

Contents

Preface

WHEN a handful of us organized the Adams County Historical society ten years ago in Hastings, Nebraska, we didn't dream that it could develop into a delightful life. For that is what it has become—a way of living, really, wherein we think, plan, talk, even dream, about local history.

Even when we are away from our home territory, each of us seems to gravitate into whatever historical society is around, just to find out what's going on there!

The suggestions and advice contained in this *Primer for Local Historical Societies* come from our successes, and failures, and from those of other societies we've seen at close hand. They are the result of ten years of study and the good advice of such professionals as Gary Gore and May Dean Eberling, who helped with the Preservation and Restoration chapters.

This book is written for a historical society which, like ours, is short on money, but long on enthusiasm, imagination and ingenuity, and is geographically remote from professional help and advice. It is written for the group that will rely on volunteer labor, will have to spend much time raising money through various means, and will not know the meaning of the word *Impossible*. It is written for the society which will contribute harmony and cohesiveness to the community as it preserves local history.

Before You Organize: In the Beginning . . .

Why do you want to have a historical society? What functions, what purposes, do you have in mind?

Do you see it as a museum, housing collections of furniture, kitchen utensils, clothing, artifacts of the past, showing this generation how another generation lived?

Or as a library, housing photographs, newspapers, documents, diaries and scrapbooks, manuscripts and tape recordings, providing research materials, telling this generation how another generation lived?

Or as a site-marking group, locating exact places where significant events of the past took place, telling exactly who lived, or fought, or invented what here?

Or as the restoration of a fine old building or cluster of buildings, recreated to show precisely how another generation lived, with the furniture, leaded windows, floor coverings and auxiliary pieces in place?

Or as a publishing group, researching and printing stories about the past, distributing them to members and others?

Chances are you have a combination of purposes in mind when you begin. Decide what are the most urgent needs in your community for a historical society to fill, what are the inclinations of the people who will be your members, and what are

1

the financing possibilities of the group. You will probably need to establish a list of priorities if you want to accomplish a number of purposes.

What is your scope?

Will it be general in its history, preserving material from all periods of the historic past, or will it be specific? If your community was most active in the Revolutionary era, will your society concentrate on that period? Or if it was most active during the Confederacy, will you concentrate on that? If the significance of your area was greatest during the pioneer days, or during the development of the atomic bomb, will you limit your attention to either of those periods?

Or will it be limited to a particular trade or profession? Will your society specialize in preserving material only about coal mining, or sugar-beet growing, or automobile production?

Will it be limited to a specific function, as a Columbia University Historical Society?

Or will it be limited to a particular racial or ethnic group—a historical society for Blacks, Chicanos, or Germans from Russia?

Most historical societies, particularly ones organized in and by a community rather than a specialized group, are general in scope, tending to focus on all of the historic past in the geographic area—the history of Smith County, for instance, or of Brownville. They may have more material on one period than another—there may be more furniture, knickknacks, pictures and clippings from the Victorian era than from the 1920s—but most local historical societies tend to be all-inclusive historically, preserving materials from all periods.

If yours is an all-inclusive society, do not ever overlook the fact that what happens today will soon be a part of history, and that the in-between years are even now a part of history. The old days are glamorous and exciting, simply because they are alien; we can remember what happened yesterday and it doesn't seem historical. But last year's high school annual will be a historical document in another 20 or 50 years.

Some communities may already have museums organized, but do not have historical societies, or vice versa. The one can be organized as an adjunct to the already established institution, or may be a completely separate entity.

In some communities, for instance, the museum is financed by the town and the historical society by the county; in others, the two are contained within a single framework, with a common governing board and financial structure.

Sometimes, too, there are other already existing agencies that the historical society can work with cooperatively, their common interests and even space requirements being compatible. A case in point is a public library, which sometimes has the beginnings of a historical collection. The patrons of the library are often history buffs, and conversely, persons who enjoy history are usually great readers and users of library facilities.

There is no single procedure that is better than all others. Determine what you want to accomplish through a historical society, what is already in existence in the community, and what should be the best organizational form for you. What works well in your circumstances may not work well in others.

Do not duplicate efforts, nor set up a competing organization. Competition is great for business establishments, but not for history. History is for harmony.

Who are your members?

Will your membership be limited, open only to old-timers or First Families? Will it be open to everyone who wants to join, no matter where they were born or grew up?

If your membership is exclusive, you will necessarily limit the size of the organization, and perhaps its effectiveness.

If your membership is open to anyone who wishes to join, it can serve a useful function in the community. By crossing all sorts of sociological lines, your society will be nonpolitical, non-sectarian, nonracial, open to everyone regardless of social, economic or ethnic backgrounds.

Some communities have discovered that often newcomers are even more interested in the history of the area than some old-timers, simply because they want to know what happened there before they came. Historical societies in some communities pro-vide newcomers with packets, through the aegis of Welcome

Wagon or some similar enterprise, which include a brief history of the town, maps of historic sites in the area, sample copies of their publication, information about membership in the society and even application forms. One group, which publishes paperback books of historical stories about the region every few years, offers those books at a reduced rate to newcomers who join the society.

The membership decision is one that needs to be made early. Whether or not you have different classifications of memberships—students' for instance, or special senior citizens'—is a minor detail. The important decision is whether your membership will be open or closed.

How do you finance it?

Before you begin figuring out how you are going to finance your organization, ask yourself what you need money for.

If you plan to build or remodel something into a museum, or to restore a fine old building, or to install markers on historic sites, you need money, of course—big money, donations.

For general operational expenses, postage stamps, membership cards, letterheads, and all the rest, you'll need regular income. But what will you give your members in return for their dues?

It has happened that a few historical societies have rushed out to incorporate and collect dues—and then decided what they would do with their newfound funds. The better idea is to know exactly what your group intends to do with its resources before the membership drive begins. What will the dues be used for; what will you offer your members for their money? Will it be a series of programs with speakers telling about specific events in the history of the community; a little newspaper of local history; picnic get-togethers with speeches and games from the past? Why should anybody buy a membership in your organization?

Have a product to sell before you begin merchandising it.

Once you know what your intentions are, then decide about your dues structure. Figure out what you need money for and how many people you are likely to interest in your organization—and then decide on your dues. Henry Ford learned long ago that it's better to make a small amount of money from many people than large amounts from a few. Most local historical groups have memberships at a reasonable enough fee that anybody who wants to joint can afford to do so; membership dues usually range from $3 to $10 per family per year.

Some organizations have several different categories of membership. A family membership, for instance, entitling all of the family admission to the museum, to meetings, or to the library, may be $5 per year. Student memberships are less—$3 per year, perhaps; senior citizens' memberships, for retired persons on fixed pension incomes, are $2 or $3. There may be various categories within the family memberships, so that those who wish can pay more can become Contributing Members at $10, Patrons at $25, and Sustaining Members at $50. Use whatever nomenclature suits your particular community. Some of the lesser categories, particularly junior memberships, may be non-voting types; you will want to have that information printed on the membership cards.

Avoid the pitfall of Lifetime memberships, for those are, obviously, one-shot affairs. The 65-year-old to whom you sell one for $100 will not ever pay again, and may belong for another 25 years; you could have a regular $10 Contributing Member in him each year!

One now almost-extinct historical society in mid-America organized many years ago with the promise of single lifetime memberships of $100 per family. When the money came in there was lots; the society erected a number of site markers. Then the money was gone. It was a closed-membership group, with only First Families allowed in it—there were no other eligible members; the society, for a while active and aggressive, is now all but nonexistent.

Membership dues will provide the regular bread-and-butter money you need for normal operating costs. But what about money for major investments?

To build a museum or restore an old mansion or publish a comprehensive history, you will need large sums of money, more than you can accumulate through membership dues. Further chapters in this book, dealing with those specific subjects, will give suggestions on special fund-raising techniques.

Where do you get help?

All sorts of help is available for local historical societies. The most obvious place is your state historical society, whose addresses are given in Appendix A. Another excellent source is the American Association for State and Local History, 1400 Eighth Avenue South, Nashville, Tennessee, 37203, has a variety of books and technical leaflets available on specific subjects. Lists of publications pertinent to the subject are given at the end of the chapters that follow.

The AASLH has consultant services available, sending specialists in various fields to historical societies for short periods of time to give professional help.

Through talking with other historical agencies of all kinds, and working with them, you will gain expertise, as you will also by cooperating with other agencies in your community.

How do you begin?

As soon as you are reasonably sure that you are ready to start, fix a date and time and place for a meeting. Obviously you and others in the community have discussed the possibility of organizing a historical society. But there may be many other people who are also interested but whose identities you do not know.

Use all available means of publicity to get the word out that a historical society is to be organized. Send well-written stories to the newspapers in your area, both weeklies and dailies and shoppers' guides; send them to the state historical society in time for their newsletters; send them to local radio and television stations. Have announcements made in history classes in the local schools, at community meetings such as Rotary, church groups, country clubs, union meetings. Pin up notices at the local grocery store and launderette. Saturate the community with information about the organization of a historical society, being sure that the date, time and place of the organizational meeting are clear.

Sometimes it's possible to use some special cause or event to coordinate the founding of a society—the one hundredth anniversary of the town, for instance, or the visit of a high dignitary from far away, or the reestablishment of the town band after many years of inactivity. You can combine your publicity efforts and make more colorful stories than just the beginning of a society could provide. You will have to make it clear, though, that although the occasion may be fleeting, the society is not; it is not a onetime thing but a permanent, continuing institution.

You Organize

The nucleus group which is organizing your historical society should draft a constitution and simple by-laws, outlining the purposes of the group, lists of officers and directors, their duties and tenure, and times of regular meetings. As with all legal documents, the simpler the better; if your by-laws are too restrictive, they will have to be changed often.

Sample constitutions and by-laws are given in *Organizing a Local Historical Society* by Clement M. Silvestro, published by the American Association for State and Local History; your state historical society may also have some model by-laws for you.

In fact, it would be to your advantage to interest a good lawyer and a good accountant in becoming involved in your organization; they may be able to steer you away from possible difficulties. Businessmen can give practical advice. And if there is a newspaper reporter who is interested, you have ready-made help with publicity stories.

Try to enlist the help of people who have energy, enthusiasm, imagination and expertise in specialized fields; yours will be an organization dependent upon volunteer workers, and you need as many people with expert knowledge as possible. Encourage people you know will work and will follow through on their promises to join the society; you will need all kinds of willing, dedicated helpers.

It is true that you need somebody to pour tea at the tea party (and to provide the teapot), but you need even more bodies to wash teacups in the kitchen! Have as varied a group of historically-minded members as you can find. Your group can represent a broad spectrum in the community, people from many professions, economic levels and social strata; with a common interest in history, you can make friends of people you have never met before. It will include all ages, too, for the youngsters may be among the most enthusiastic members. Children understand what is real and what isn't, and are the least hooked by unprovable legends. The historical society may be the only place in the community where the young and the old will come together in an appreciation of what each group has to contribute to the whole.

At the first meeting, elect officers and directors. Presumably you will have settled the slate fairly well before the meeting, but don't have it hard and fast and inflexible. Someone you've not thought of may show up at that first meeting and be intensely interested, with much imagination and vigor to add to the group. Have your directorate representative of the community, not an established clique.

Your by-laws will have established provisions for continuity in the society, and will have provided for consistent change in leadership so that office-holding doesn't become locked into a particular group. All of your officers will be aware of their terms of office from the beginning.

Your two most important officers at first will be the president, who represents the organization to the public, oversees all of the planning, appoints members to various committees, and keeps track of what is going on in all parts of the organization, and the treasurer, who is in charge of all fund-collecting, bill-paying and other financial matters, and custodian of legal documents.

The secretary will take minutes of your meetings and keep track of the activities of the group in official minute books. You may have such other officers as you feel you need to carry out the purposes of the society; all of the officers will automatically become members of the board of directors.

The directors will plan and implement all of the activities of the organization; they are the policy-makers, responsible for decisions about long-range goals. As the title implies, they direct. They are more involved with general, overall aims than with specific day-to-day procedures.

Separate committees will be charged with the specific functions of the organizations. What they are will depend upon the purposes of the society. For instance, if your group is interested in site-marking, you will have a committee responsible for that activity; if the society plans to develop tours of historic sites in the area, you will have a tour committee. The committee functions and memberships will change through the years as you enlarge some activities, perhaps finish others.

Because it is likely that at first you will not have a permanent location for your historical society, but will possibly be operating out of members' homes, it is wise to rent a post office box for continuity of mailing address. As you change officers through the years, the number of the post office box remains the same and is a permanent mailing address.

The treasurer will establish a bank account to make all of the financial transactions of the society by check; cancelled checks are far easier to keep track of than are receipts. The by-laws will establish whether checks will need more than one signature on them and if so, whose.

You will also want to rent a safety-deposit box in a bank as a repository for such legal documents as your constitution and by-laws, incorporation papers listing your nonprofit status, and other significant papers. Through the years, as you change officers you will also change the names at the post office and bank, authorizing individuals who have access to the post office box and the safety-deposit box.

As soon as you possibly can, incorporate as a nonprofit institution so that gifts—antiques, documents, pictures, cash, or others—can be deducted on donors' income tax return forms. Also, secure a letter of determination from the Internal Revenue Service which certifies your tax-exempt status. With your registered nonprofit status, you also have access to various state and federal grants and foundation funds, if you wish to go after any of them. (Make sure these documents are secured in a safe place;

it might be well to have Xerox copies made so that you have duplicates available in the president's files and possibly others.)

Have membership cards available at all meetings. Do all that you can to stimulate persons to join your society, and make it easy for them to do so.

After you have the officers and directors duly elected and settled into office, have a modest amount of office supplies printed. These will include membership cards, as much letterhead paper as you think you will use for a year or so, membership-due bills, gift certificate cards, documents acknowledging receipt of gifts, and appropriate envelopes.

Your office printing will be far more effective if you use the same kind of type for all of it, varying only in size. If you have a

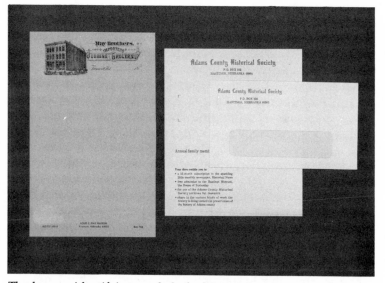

The logo or identifying symbol of a historical society can take many forms. The Louis E. May Museum in Fremont, Nebraska, is housed in the restored residence of a merchant; reproductions of his old billing forms are used for letterheads, an imaginative blending of the old and the new. Even if you use stock type from your printer for your logo be sure to use it in all of your printed material so that the public will immediately identify your historical society with the type.

member who is an artist or draftsmen, who can draw an attractive design (*logo* is the specialized word) signifying the historical society, you will have a distinctive symbol or trademark. Otherwise, pick a particular kind of type from the sample type book and use that same kind for all of your printing needs.

Your office supplies need not be expensive—you do not want to overload your budget with this minor operational expenditure—but they should reflect stability so that the public considers your historical society one of substance and permanence. The list, of course, will include carbon paper, for whoever takes care of the correspondence will file carbon copies of all letters, along with copies of all publications—even informal flyers—for the society's own records.

You are organized, you have officers and members—now what do you do? What do you offer your members? A program.

At an early meeting, perhaps the first after you organize, have a program about the history of the community or whatever is the concern of your historical society.

The speaker can be a knowledgeable local person, or can be an imported "authority" from somewhere else. Because, as you know, a prophet is without honor in his own country, your audience will probably react better to an Expert from Far Away than to someone they know and see every day.

If there are controversial issues in the community's history —and you may be surprised to discover that there are—an outside expert can help avoid an immediate split into factions.

Someone from the state historical society may be available to speak for a reasonable fee plus travel costs. Or the state group may be able to suggest someone else who is acknowledged as an authority on your local history.

The program should concentrate on a specific subject, not just the history of the community generally; ask the lecturer to give factual material (dates, vital statistics, names) and colorful details (legends, specifics on how the people lived and played and dressed and made their living) during the time under consideration in the lecture.

For instance, if your community was especially active during

A brand-new historical society took over one corner of the city library, using display cases to exhibit pictorial matter and filing cases for its archival material. Within 5 years, this historical society had outgrown these quarters.

the Civil War days, the lecture topic could cover how the community lived when the soldiers were gone to war: how the women got in and out of buggies and wagons wearing hoop skirts, how they managed the family business, or what songs or ditties little children composed and sang and some of the games they played.

If your community has sod houses in its history, you could have a program on how to build a sod house, with specifics on how the houses were furnished, how the bedbugs thrived, how the housewives lived in semidarkness and used potted plants for colorful relief.

If your community lived through the dust-bowl days, you could hear about the causes of the dust storms, details about dust pneumonia, a description of the color of the sky, the intensity of the wind, and the aftermath of the storm when housewives had to scoop the grit from their windowsills.

The topic should be colorful, thought-provoking, specific —and most of all, historical. It should be something the audience can relate to, either from personal experience or lore passed down to them from other generations. It should excite thought and memories and spark their imaginations.

If your speaker has a prepared speech, be sure to secure a copy of it for your own files. If he doesn't, then get his permission beforehand to tape-record the speech and all of the remarks that people may make from the audience afterward; have the tape transcribed later into typewritten form for your files. This is valuable history; preserve it.

If your long-range interest is in establishing a museum or a library, at the time you publicize this meeting you could ask for display materials pertaining to the subject—photographs, artifacts, old diaries or journals. Then put them on display in the lecture room or somewhere nearby to add interest to the program before and after the speech. (Your secretary could take notes of what items are there and in whose possession they are, so that later on, when you are in a situation to use them for your museum or library, you will know what is available, and where.)

Your first meeting needs careful planning and the use of much imagination and ingenuity to attract and keep the attention of people you want to work in your historical society.

OTHER HELP AVAILABLE

Organizing a Local Historical Society by Clement M. Silvestro. Published by the American Association for State and Local History. Contains sample constitutions and by-laws.

AASLH Technical Leaflet 37, *Recruiting Members*.

AASLH Technical Leaflet 72, *The Role of Trustees: Selection and Responsibilities*.

Financing

No matter what your programs are, you will need some sort of financing to carry them out. Where will it come from?

Memberships

Have membership on an annual basis, so that you have a continuing source of income for your operational expenses. The amount you charge will depend upon what you have to offer your members—what you have to sell, and upon the affluence of your members—and what the traffic will bear.

You may wish to have different categories of memberships. For instance, Historic Denver, Inc., has this annual membership structure:

$5,000	Benefactor	$100	Supporting
2,500	Patron	50	Associate
1,000	Associate Patron	25	Participating
500	Contributing	10	Introductory
250	Sustaining	5	Student (nonvoting).

Smaller, less affluent communities would want to scale the membership dues structure downward, and perhaps add a category for senior citizens, and perhaps a nonresident membership.

For an historical society in a smaller community, perhaps the dues structure could be as follows:

$100	Patron	$5	Regular Member
50	Friend	3	Senior Citizen or Nonresident Member
25	Contributor	2	Student Member

It would be advantageous for you to have a ruling, either from an accountant or from the Internal Revenue Service, to ascertain whether contributions beyond the regular $5 membership—or whatever your basic membership fee is—would be tax deductible.

Do not have your dues structure so high that you scare off possible members. And do not try to bully members into moving to a higher bracket; you may lose them altogether. Some historical societies charge a flat, overall fee of say, $3 or $5 per family per year, figuring that through volume they make more than they would with escalating fees.

Do not overlook the fact that many people who have lived in your community during their growing-up years but have since moved away may be interested in your society from a nostalgic point of view. This interest will be particularly great if you have any sort of publishing program, wherein you can mail them material that may remind them of their earlier years. High school alumni lists and old school annuals are good sources of names.

City or county support

Many historical societies receive mill levies or outright grants from city or county boards. Some states have passed legislation making it possible for cities or counties to assess mill levies for the support of local historical societies. Check with your state historical society to find out the situation in your state.

If and when you appear before the city council or village board or county commissioners to ask for financial support, plan your performance in some detail in advance. Get in touch with the obvious leaders of the board well ahead of time and discuss with them your chances of getting financial support; there is no point in appearing before them and being turned down if there is no hope of success. (You do not want a history of failure for your historical society.) If they feel that you have a chance of funding, discuss what would be the best time for your appearance; the day the board is discussing a ticklish zoning problem or some other touchy question would not be a good time tactically for you to ask for money. When you have affirmative indications, then ask to have your name placed on the agenda.

Prepare a succinct, carefully-worded paper listing why you need money, what your programs are, and why it would be advantageous to that group to fund you. When you are seeking public funds, it is essential that you explain that what you are doing will serve the entire public; if you yourself are convinced that an active historical society will stimulate pride in the community, draw tourists to it to spend money, and develop a continuity within it, then it is not hard to put it into words when you ask for money.

Many boards prefer to have this material presented to them in writing before the meeting, so they can consider it at their leisure; if so, get the typewriter and the duplicating machine busy. Be businesslike; be factual, rather than flowery. When you appear before the board, be prepared to answer questions—and to be brief. If you feel that you may run into some opposition from opposed-to-government-spending factions, arrange to have some sympathetic taxpayers in the audience, persons not obviously on your directorate but ones who would be understanding of your cause. By their presence, and by their reactions, they can add weight and authority to your plea.

The directors of one historical society spent several weeks in preparation for their appearance before a county board, even practicing "If he says this, I say that . . . " To their astonishment, the request was granted in 60 seconds, with the question, "Why haven't you come here before this?" The directors were left, happily, with many undelivered speeches in their heads. They had done their homework with the board well ahead of the meeting.

Entrance fees

Although ideally a museum should be free to anyone who wants to visit it, especially when the community is contributing to its collections, many museums feel that they must establish entrance fees as a means of obtaining additional funds.

If your museum is contemplating such a procedure, realize in advance that the entrance fees cannot possibly be large enough to pay for large capital expenditures, but merely provide part of the operating costs. Do not set your fees so high that nobody will come to your museum; you want people to visit it, not be kept away because they cannot afford to come in.

Some small museums have a poor-box arrangement at the door, so that visitors either coming in or going out will drop contributions of money into the basket or jar or whatever. This arrangement does raise some revenue, all right, but certainly not as much as a standard admission fee. If you have such an arrangement, make sure a casual passerby cannot take the money out!

If you have county or city mill-levy support for your museum, you may be enjoined from charging an entrance fee. Be sure to check this legal detail before you make an error.

Assorted money-raising projects

There are as many other money-raising possibilities as there are cornstalks in the field; you are limited only by your imagination and energy. For instance:

Hold flea markets or garage sales.

Benefit style shows of costumes of long ago can be profitable. Include narration telling something of the history of each era represented by the clothing.

Stage an old-time carnival or fair, with booths, games of chance (if they are legal in your state), exhibits, feats of strength, and other sideshows. This is a chance for the use of much ingenuity, the utilization of much social history in detail, and for tremendous community cooperation; it is especially good for a small community.

Sponsor handicraft sales, on a year-round basis. If there is a local crafts organization, you can combine with it, or with individual craftsmen, to sell their hand-made products—quilts, knitted goods, cornhusk dolls, whittled wooden items, wrought-

A fashion show which describes history through clothing of the past is a means of raising money for a local historical society. The narration should describe how people lived, the setting of the town, and give other historical data, as well as point out peculiarities of the old-fashioned clothing.

iron objects—on a shared-profit basis. You can supply the original patterns for them, securing them from old books or original models.

Collect, print, and sell cookbooks of old recipes indigenous to the area, either those brought by early settlers or those evolved by the first residents there. Concentrate on your historic wealth; if your community was active during the Revolutionary War days, get recipes for cranberry shrub, Indian pudding and other native dishes; if your community was established at the time of the Civil War, get recipes for dishes common then. Cookbooks always sell well, and before long you will have made enough to pay the printer, so that all the sales after that are clear profit. (Price your book at least at three times its cost to you.)

Organize benefit card parties, with those in attendance wearing costumes of long ago.

Sell postcards or note sheets year-round which picture something relating to the history of the area.

Request community service clubs, such as Rotary, Kiwanis, Lions, or others, for continuing support of a specified amount per year.

Print and sell coloring books for youngsters with basic line drawings of historic places in the community, of historic characters, or other topics suggested by the story of your community. Perhaps junior or senior high school students could help you decide what pictures would be appealing to youngsters as well as historically accurate; if there is an accomplished artist in the schools, that student could prepare the sketches.

Productions of old-time drama, with the supplemental attractions that were common historically, are engrossing for both participants and viewers. Check old newspapers to find out what kinds of dramatic presentations were given. If these can be given in an old-fashioned setting, with lanterns and other historically accurate accoutrements, they are even more effective. (Do, however, use restraint on an Old-Fashioned Mellerdrammer, with peanut tossing at the villain; don't ham it up too much!)

Get the name of the historical society in wills, and as the beneficiary of memorial gifts.

Fancy hand-sewn articles can be made for sale at museum and society gift shops, or at crafts sales. One historical society produced "historic" gift wrap from advertisements in old newspapers and magazines.

There are many more possibilities, too, all of them requiring time and energy to work out; the ones which relate in some way to the specific history of the area are the most worthwhile and significant, for they not only contribute revenue to your treasury but they also draw attention to the historic wealth of your community.

State and federal grants for specific projects

For specific programs, not for continuing operations, some state and federal funds are available. These funds are generally for projects that an organization would otherwise not be able to perform. The grants are not available for usual operating costs, going only to well-established groups with a record of accomplishment.

The National Endowment for the Humanities and state Humanities committees, the National Endowment for the Arts and state Arts agencies, are logical starting points in the search for funds. Each group on the national level endorses support to museums and historical societies for specific projects. On the state level, it is often possible to coordinate your activities with the particular program your state agency is encouraging for that fiscal year.

Names and addresses of state arts and humanities groups are given in Appendix B. If you think you have a special project which might fall into the purview of either group, write to the state agencies requesting copies of their guidelines and procedural manuals.

Study the programs carefully to see if their guidelines suggest a project you can do within your society which fulfills your requirements—and theirs. For instance, one state Humanities committee focused its program one year on ethnic groups; a local historical society saw that as a means of sponsoring a series of programs on the ethnic backgrounds of the community. The society worked out a significant project to study the diverse historical-cultural background of the community and to gain a greater understanding of the town.

In another situation, a local historical society was able to secure some funding from the state-based Arts group for preservation and presentation of historic old movies to local audiences.

Not all state-based agencies are organized to handle proposals of local historical groups, but it certainly is worth the effort it takes to make inquiries.

The National Endowments for the Arts and for the Humanities are interested in projects which are significant on a national level, and sometimes will consider proposals from local groups which are innovative and possible pilot projects. Their address is Washington, D.C., 20506.

History News, the monthly publication of the American Association for State and Local History, has a page every other month or so, entitled "Dateline: Washington," which gives information about specific funding on the federal level, listing general guidelines and giving addresses and deadline dates.

If you are considering filing proposal applications with either state or the national agencies, be forewarned that you must plan ahead at least a year, sometimes more. Application deadlines are always many months in advance of the actual starting dates, and are rigid. Staff members of these agencies will be eager to help you, to make suggestions, to work out arrangements whereby you can adapt your projects to their guidelines. Follow their guidelines, and meet the deadlines.

Learn to write applications, keeping them simple, honest, enthusiastic. Pay particular attention to the budget page; you will need to make sure that you have adequate matching funds. (Learn to distinguish between *hard-match* i.e., actual cash and *soft-match*, which is in-kind services.) Many government funding projects require that you have as much money to match as that you are asking for; you can therefore, usually ask for only half as much as the project will cost, supplying the other half from other funds.

There are some other sources of funding from state and federal sources. Your state historical society may be able to suggest them to you. One word of caution: it is easy sometimes to stray from the field, to become so entranced by funding possibilities that you lose sight of your ultimate goal. Always keep in mind that you are a historical society and that your primary purposes are the accumulation and preservation of data and artifacts and the interpretation and dissemination of data.

Foundations

Another source of funds is foundation money. There are several thousand foundations in the United States which by law must dispense a certain portion of their income each year to nonprofit organizations.

Many of them are small, with local or regional connections; they are often the ones most likely to support local historical societies. How to find out about them, their names and addresses, is sometimes difficult. Your local library may have books listing foundations.

There are eight regional collections of current foundation information. Those names and addresses are given in Appendix C. The foundation directories will indicate the kind of projects each one is primarily interested in.

For smaller trusts, consult the trust officers at your local bank for names of trusts too small to make the published lists; they can tell you something of the interests they have.

Do not write to foundations which seem to have no interest in your type of work. When you write a letter to a foundation, briefly describe the project and your tentative request, asking if that organization would be interested in supporting it. The formal application should be made only if the foundation indicates interest in your project.

Your applications to foundations should be clear, concise, brief and convincing. Tell exactly how much money you need, what you need the money for, and how your service will benefit the community. Since all foundations have many requests for grants, be prepared for polite, but definite refusals.

In addition to foundations, some corporations will give funding for specific projects as part of their public relations effort. These are primarily one-shot projects which allow them visibility, that is, an opportunity to have their name before the public. For a museum, for instance, it could be a display case with a discreet brass plaque saying, "This display case contributed by the Zilch Department Store," or a line in a catalog saying "Printing of this catalog made possible by the None-such Manufacturing Company." Some major corporations, such as IBM, will match employees' gifts; if you have enough paid employees to make such an inquiry plausible, that means could be used to augment your income.

Audits

No matter your size and your sources of funding, if you can possibly arrange an audit each year, do so. Some grant proposals require you to submit an audited financial report, but whether you're forced to it or not, it is a businesslike procedure. You will want to be businesslike, as well as historical.

OTHER HELP AVAILABLE

Finances and Fund Raising, by Leslie H. Fishel, Jr., tape cassette. American Association for State and Local History.
AASLH Technical Leaflet 62, *Securing Grant Support*.

Publicity

To carry out your work effectively, you will need the help of all available publicity. The public needs to know what you are doing in order to appreciate your work and to join with you in accomplishing it.

How to work with the news media

Most newspaper staffs as well as other news media, alas, rely heavily on prepared news releases; they are far more likely to run your stories if you provide ready-to-use material rather than asking for a reporter to cover an event. If you do not have a skilled newspaper reporter in your membership, then you will have to assign somebody to learn the basics of reporting and news-writing.

When you have a story about some forthcoming event, write it up in acceptable newspaper style, telling the most important facts first, and including who, what, when, where, why and how, in the first paragraph. Be accurate, and spell all the names correctly. The story should be typed, double-spaced, with a large margin at the top and adequate margins at each side. Always provide the name and phone number of the person who wrote it, so that the newspaper can make follow-up contact.

Be sure you know the deadlines for the local newspaper, and for the local radio and television stations. If you want the story in a particular issue of the newspaper or on a particular day on local radio or television, have the story in the office well ahead of the deadline. Many newspapers will be more likely to give your story good space if you do not specify a particular day for an advance story, but indicate that you want it to run some time prior to a given date. (Wednesday is grocery-ad day for many daily newspapers, for instance, and there is more news space available in those fatter issues.)

Many weekly newspapers are printed at a central offset printing shop and have deadlines several days in advance; for Thursday newspapers, for instance, the deadline for copy usually is Monday.

Perhaps there are specific columns in which you can have reminders: social calendars, or Next-Week-In-Town, or something similar. Utilize all of the news space you possibly can to tell about your planned activities.

Many local or regional radio and television stations have community calendars which list events of the day. Write your paragraph convincingly—you need to sell your meeting—and be sure to list the who, what, when, and where; send the story to the Community Calendar, or whatever it is called, with the notation of which day or days you wish it read.

Local stations often have daytime community service interviews that allow you time to interpret the purposes of your historical society. It might be possible for you to set up a schedule of appearances every 3 months or at regular intervals, at least, with different individuals from the group appearing each time to explain different functions of the group.

Study your own situation carefully. What are the means by which persons in your community learn about events? What columns do they read, what local television and radio news programs are the most likely to carry your news?

After a meeting at which officers were elected, or volunteers given achievement pins, or some other newsworthy event took place, write the story and get it to the news media immediately for their use; after an event has happened, the story must be in the newsroom as soon as possible—it is no longer news if you wait. Be sure all the names are spelled correctly, and the occasion, place, and other significant information is given.

If you have had a particularly stimulating address, either write it up in précis form, quoting directly the most salient points, or send a copy of the speech, with the most interesting sentences underlined, to the newspaper office, along with a paragraph telling what the event was, where, when, who the speaker was, and how many people attended. Make it easy for the local news media to use your material.

If you have a particularly significant story you think is of statewide importance or more, suggest to the local news editor that he put it on the Associated Press or United Press International wire. If he does not concur, do not argue with him.

When you have a story you think the newspaper or local television station would like to use with pictures, telephone the news editor well in advance so that he can schedule a photographer and reporter to cover the event. Describe the happening and why you think it is worth pictorial coverage, and let him make the decision; if he decides negatively, do not wheedle or threaten—if you do, you'll have no chance another time!

Establish a good rapport with the local editors of the news media; if you display a professionalism about your work with them they will respect you and will cooperate with you. If you can get a reporter assigned to do an interpretive story at the very beginning of the society, you will have a supporter and interpreter forever; if you cannot, be as helpful as you can to any member of the press you will work with.

How to utilize other sources

There are other means of publicity, too: posters displayed in store windows, especially grocery stores, and bulletin boards in shopping centers and launderettes; announcements in history classes and at club meetings of all kinds in the community; signboards on banks or other institutions in town. If you meet in a building belonging to a particular group—a church, a women's club, a grange hall—be sure its members know about you.

If you are having a membership drive, or a significant event far enough in the future that timing isn't essential, you can check

A ladies' book club turned over to a local historical society its files of yearbooks dating back almost 100 years. Because of the society's rapport with the local newspaper, it was able to have a photographer and reporter present; this picture and a large story appeared in the newspaper the next day. Many other groups learned of the work and the needs of the historical society. Publicity takes many forms; be alert to all opportunities to publicize your work.

with various institutions and then have brochures printed or mimeographed to be included in billings which the telephone company, the utility company, the bank or department stores mail out. You and your volunteers may have to help stuff the envelopes, but those mailings are a good way of reaching many people. If you make arrangements in advance, grocery stores will often stuff those printed sheets in bags at the checkout stand.

Study carefully the means by which people in your community learn about what's going on. If it's a party-line telephone, use that; if it's some other means, use that! Saturate your community with information about your historical society.

OTHER HELP AVAILABLE

AASLH Technical Leaflet 45, *Newspaper Publicity*.
AASLH Technical Leaflet 26, *Reading Your Public through Television*.
AASLH Technical Leaflet 3, *Effective Public Relations*.
AASLH Technical Leaflet 29, *Turning Travelers into Visitors*.

Beginning Projects for Limited Budgets

The accumulation and preservation of data and artifacts, and the interpretation and dissemination of data are the primary purposes of historical societies.

To accumulate, preserve, interpret and dissiminate that history, you must make the community aware of it; aware, interested, proud of it, and involved with you in it. In its work, a historical society can bring unity and harmony to a community, attracting the talents and energies of widely diverse groups and individuals, working together in a common cause. Many historical societies have discovered that in their study of the past, they have stimulated their communities to a better present.

If yours is like most beginning historical societies, you will be long on ideas, imagination, and enthusiasm—and short on cash. Here are some suggestions for beginning projects. They are simple, involve little financial outlay but considerable hard work and attention to detail, and serve the dual function of gathering and preserving history and of getting the community as a whole interested in the history of the area.

Meetings with speakers talking about local history

A good beginning project would be to have a series of meetings at regularly scheduled times, perhaps once a month, at which specific speakers deliver well-researched, detailed papers on definite subjects of local interest. The time should be limited to about 30 minutes per paper, with no more than two papers per meeting; the speakers should indicate in their manuscripts the sources of their information, although they would not read those aloud as they present their papers.

The subjects should be strictly limited in scope. The ethnic culture programs mentioned above could suggest some topics. If your community had large groups of Swedish immigrants, or Bohemians, or others, you might consider studying them. Why did they leave their homeland, and when; why did they come to this particular area; did they come as family groups, as individuals, or whole colonies? What did they do for a living when they first came here, what have been their contributions to the community? There may be ethnic clubs or churches right in the area that would like to participate or help out. There could be enough material here for a number of programs.

Perhaps someone in the community has old letters or diaries for source material; the interviewing of old-timers and the scanning of old newspapers might turn up more. Perhaps some local genealogists could fill in some details for you. Let the audience add details, too.

One local group engendered so much enthusiasm with its ethnic culture programs that afterward some of the participants organized a society of Germans from Russia, and others, a French-Canadian historical club, both new associations working closely with the historical society. In future years, the off-shoot clubs will be able to provide programs themselves for the parent organization.

Other subjects could relate to specific industries: for instance, if yours is a manufacturing area, find out what attracted the first industries to the region, and when, what the first ones were, and how the various industries have changed through the years. You will probably discover that you have unearthed material that the companies themselves do not know about. You could have a program on industries that are no longer in existence. You might have a whole series of programs, one on each specific industry.

If yours is a tobacco-producing area, then how about a pro-

An interestingly-presented, well-prepared speech on a definite subject of historical interest can provide a fascinating program for a local historical society. The topic should be specific, the speech well worked out in advance, and if time permits, the audience may be invited to participate afterward by adding historical nuggets of their own.

gram on the history of tobacco-growing. Why did the early farmers decide to grow tobacco, and when; what have been the different varieties through the years; how have production methods changed; who have been some of the influential planters; and what have been some of the problems? The more detail you can give, the more colorful you can make your presentation, the more interest listeners will show. One prairie historical society sponsored a lecture by a collector of barbed wire, who gave an intriguing study on the different kinds of barbed wire used by the early pioneers of the area; a western historical society asked a gun collector to speak on Guns That Won the West, and a group of goggle-eyed little boys sat on the front row listening to every word!

The topics are endless. You can think of dozens—circuses of the past, the old ice house, bootlegging, intriguing murder cases or bank robberies, livery barns and horse races, crystal-set radios: just ask yourself what you would like to know about your community. The programs can be given by knowledgeable members of your own society, representatives from collectors's or hobby clubs, out-of-towners, or by anybody. Who gives them is not important; they should simply be worthwhile additions to your overall knowledge of the past.

When you plan your programs, check to be sure your community has resources available for the necessary research on the topics assigned. If not, find out where such material is available, and whether it is possible to have a member go there—to the state historical society or even further. Whatever your topics are, you will want to make sure that they are well researched and the material is presented accurately. If you do not have access to sufficient resource material, change the topics.

Be sure to save copies of the speeches for your permanent files. Tape-record them, too, after you have asked the speaker for his permission. With each program, you might have exhibits of pictures, documents, artifacts, maps and other historical memorabilia to illustrate the lecture.

That is a passive sort of program, in that only a few people do the work and the rest are spectators. As you build up the confidence and techniques, you can start planning some projects that call for more member participation.

Locating historical information

Since the accumulation of data is one of the primary purposes of your historical society, searching out that information provides a good project to concentrate on in the early years of the organization.

What material has already been published about your area? Where are copies located? And what is in it? You will want to prepare a list of what is available, and where it is—Bibliographies and indexes.

Bibliographies

A *bibliography* is a list of books about a given subject, and even though you may not have copies of those books themselves, to know that they exist, what is in them, and where they are located, is most useful information.

In the late 1800s many regional histories were published by commercial printing establishments, most of whom financed their books by selling space in them for biographical or business information. Was your community included? In the early 1900s, there was another rash of commercially printed local histories. Were you included?

What state histories have been written about your state, and how much is in them about your community? What pamphlets have been published—some from the Chamber of Commerce, for instance? What school histories have been written, or histories of churches in your community?

A good starting point to local historical information is your state historical library. Spend time there, talking to the librarian and going through the card catalog to find out what material that particular library lists in its files.

Check the books themselves to see what is in them of particular significance to your society. Make lists, including the name of the book, author, publisher, date—and what is of interest to your group.

Say that you are the Fairfield, Nebraska, Historical Society. You find one particular volume, published in 1890, which contains material about Fairfield. Your entry would look like this:

——————— (No author listed), *Biographical and Historical Memoirs of Adams, Clay, Webster and Nuckolls Counties of Nebraska*, The Goodspeed Publishing Company, Chicago, 1890. Clay County, Chapter XIX, pp. 341-363. Population, Elevations, Area, Rivers and Streams, Physical Formations, Grasshopper Plagues, Effect of Same, Storms and Blizzards. Chapter XX, Fairfield Journals and Periodicals, pp. 365-366; G.A.R. and Militia Lists, Fairfield, pp. 369-370. Chapter XXIV, pp. 387-530. Fairfield, Pre-emption of Town Sites, Original Surveys, Incorporation, Early Merchants, Pioneer Businessmen, First Buildings, Mayors, Commercial Interests, Fires, Water System, Educational and Religious Matters, Secret and Benevolent Organizations, General History."

You would go through all the other pertinent books in the state historical library to see what other references are made to Fairfield, and would make similar listings, in each case indicating that a copy of the book is located in the Nebraska State Historical Society library.

Check all sorts of magazines, too, using the Readers Guide and any other reference works; the state historical quarterly, the state department of commerce or tourism or highways publications, or corporate magazines may have had stories in them about Fairfield. What material is in them, what are the dates and volume numbers of the magazines, and where are they located? All this information comprises your bibliography.

Indexes

At some time you would go back over that same material to make more detailed lists, according to subject matter, indexing your material. From the Goodspeed volume of 1890, for instance, you would list "Newspaper, Fairfield, _____ (No author listed), *Biographical and Historical Memoirs of Adams, Clay, Webster, and Nuckolls Counties of Nebraska*, pp. 365-366." Under the newspaper listing, you would enter any other references, from other books, to newspapers in Fairfield. Whenever anyone wanted to find information about early-day newspapers in Fairfield, the card catalog index card "Newspapers" would list the books, the page numbers, and the locations of each book which refers to newspapers.

Indexing of information is a long, time-consuming project, and will require the time and talent of many members of your group over a long period of time. But it is a worthwhile undertaking.

Members of your own historical society will possibly have historical volumes of their own; ask them to make similar listings from their own books, indicating what material is in them and where the books are located—entries for both your bibliographical listing and for your index. When you are doing research on a specific subject, you will then be able to tell quickly what material is available, and where to find it.

If churches or schools in your area have celebrated anniversaries—their one hundredth, especially—perhaps they published pamphlets or booklets. Who has them? What is in them? Try to locate them and make listings of their contents.

Who in your community keeps scrapbooks, and what is in them of historic interest? You can do the same sort of indexing and listing for them as for books. Where are old school annuals located?

Local newspapers are probably the best source of all. Your newspaper office may contain a morgue of clippings about various subjects. If it is a small newspaper office, perhaps the editor will let you make listings of subjects, particularly if the clippings go back into the past so that you will know what material is there. Offer the editor help in organizing or maintaining the morgue, if need be; such service will help both of your institutions.

Where are old newspaper of your community kept, either originals or microfilm copies? You won't start out making an index of stories in them—you will, hopefully, sometime—but at least have an indication in your files of where they are located, and the exact dates of those issues.

When you have located them, if they are not on microfilm, consider helping to get them on film. There may be money available for that purpose from the state historical society or the state library commission; check with them. The editor of the local newspaper may be more amenable to letting his papers go for awhile if the suggestion comes from local people, especially if you can explain to him that once the newspapers are on film which is located somewhere else, he won't have to tolerate persons coming into his establishment to look up old stories. In fact, he may even help you provide an inexpensive microfilm reader.

Consider the job as detective work. You are trying to find out what information is available about Fairfield, for instance, and where that information is located. You will be amazed at how your card catalog file will grow; you may start out using a shoe box but your depository will grow eventually into a bank of card drawers!

Many state historical societies, and others of similar size, have facilities to Xerox data for you, at a nominal price; if there are significant entries in volumes you know are so rare you will probably never be able to acquire copies yourself, ask to have pages duplicated for you. On your copy, be sure to indicate the exact name of the book, author, publisher, date, and other pertinent bibliographical material, as well as the page number. Material which is duplicated exactly, by any copying process, is exactly as it appeared on the original page; by utilizing this method, rather than copying in longhand, you do not run the risk of transposing figures or misspelling names.

You can involve as many people as you want in this project, assigning one person to investigate Chamber of Commerce material, another to church histories, another to scrapbooks, and even perhaps have several persons at a time go to the state historical society to work with those records. It is a job that will probably continue as long as you have an historical society! You will be adding continually to your lists.

Collecting historical material

Another project you will want to begin soon is the collecting of all kinds of historical materials—manuscripts, books, records, photographs, and other source material—and preserving them.

Use all kinds of procedures to get the word out that you are interested in collecting such material. Your own members will know it—ask them to talk to their friends; word-of-mouth is an effective means of publicizing your needs. Another is your local newspaper; if the housewives in your community are prone to "spring-cleaning," you could ask a reporter to write a clever feature story connecting the rites of spring and your need for old photographs, books and other historical material. Perhaps you could arrange an interview on the local radio station to talk about the project. Use whatever means you have at hand to publicize the fact that you are looking for source material for an historical library.

If you know that a family long-resident in the community is about to move from their home, ask them not to throw out any pictures or papers until you have had a chance to look them over. The garbage dumps of this country contain a sickening amount of history, particularly old photographs the owners did not want to keep but didn't know what to do with!

What will you want to save? Anything that pertains to the history of your area: letters describing specific events or giving details of the past; manuscripts of speeches made about the town; term papers which students have written about the community; academic dissertations—anything that adds specific historical knowledge. If the manuscripts are copyrighted, be sure they are so marked so that you will know how to handle literary rights, if you ever wish to publish any information from them.

One family recently found a little notebook in which an ancestor, back in the 1880s, had listed the various game birds he saw every day. The little notebook is now tremendously valuable, both for the historical society and for the state game commission, for it tells exactly what kinds of birds and other game were in the area then, on what days, and in what approximate quantities. They certainly are not the scientific listings of an ornithologist, but in the absence of other records, the jottings of an 11-year-old boy are important.

Old letters, journals, diaries are significant, the more so if they are clear, vivid, detailed accounts of what was taking place when they were written.

Scrapbooks—depending upon their content—may or may not be important; if they are unrelated clippings of inspirational verse, for instance, with no sources or dates indicated, they don't add to anyone's knowledge of history. (And oh, how many of those scrapbooks there were in the late 1890s!) On the other hand, scrapbooks of photographs and clippings and memorabilia —ticket stubs, programs, menus and the like—carefully labeled as to dates and events, and with each picture carefully identified, are gold-mines to historians.

Books, of course, you will want—all kinds which tell about your community. From your bibliographical lists, you will know something about what books have been published, but be on the search constantly for others. (Just because a book is old, however, it does not necessarily follow that it is valuable historically; don't save books simply because the binding is old—be sure the content is significant.) You will want to collect commemorative booklets of churches, schools, businesses; Chamber of Commerce brochures; school annuals; pamphlets issued at the time of dedication of a hospital or other public building giving architectural and background data—any books that will add to your knowledge of the community.

You will want photographs, with negatives if you can find them. Be sure that each photograph is carefully labeled when you accept it: what occasion is pictured, who are the people—their exact names, not "Mother" or "Aunt Bertha"—where is the location, when did it happen—the exact date, if possible. You may include the name of the donor, but that is not as important. (One historical society nember bought a trunkful of old pictures at an auction and discovered later that only one of the 307 was identified: it was a horse and was labeled "Beauty." The 306 others of people, places, events, are still unidentified.)

Do be careful in labeling or identifying pictures to be sure that you do not mar them. You obviously will never mark on the face of the photograph, but treat the back carefully too so that the impression of any writing does not show through. If for expendiency's sake you must write on the picture itself, make your notations lightly on the back at the very top or very bottom of the print, in an area that probably will not be reproduced if the picture is published. A better way is to type out the identification of the picture, with all of the pertinent information about it, and glue that paper to the bottom of the picture, folding the sheet over the face of the photograph when you file it. Or you can simply assign a file number, written in an inconspicuous place on the back of the picture, and then in your card catalog give a more detailed identifying description of the picture.

If your local newspaper tosses out prints of pictures after they have been published, ask if you can have those prints for your own files. After high school or other annuals have been printed, ask if you can have those photographs for your files; those paste-ups usually lie around the school for a year or so and are then thrown out, destroying good sources of pictorial history.

Establish a good rapport with the local newspaper and whatever commercial photographers work in your community to make arrangements with them for lists of their negatives, not so much of portraits as of activities they may have photographed. Then 10 years from now, if you need a picture of a particular building dedication, for instance, you will know where to locate the negative. If you can establish a friendly relationship with commercial photographers in the area, you can be of service to them when they clean out their files of negatives; you can claim some for historical purposes, sorting them and filing them in your society. Negatives should be filed in envelopes, one to an envelope, with names, occasion, location and date carefully noted on the envelope. Take the negatives out, though, before you write or type on the envelopes.

What do you do when someone loans you an old picture for a specific purpose but wants it back later? If you possibly can afford it, have a copy negative made by a commercial photographer, and a print. The duplicate may not be as sharp in detail as the original, but if it is a yellowed old print, the reproduction may turn out better than the original.

You will also want to acquire movies of your community. In your area there surely have been amateur photographers who have shot movies through the years. Locate them and acquire those you can; make listings of those you cannot obtain so that when you have sufficient funds, you can duplicate them. Movies are a startling source of social history. Even though much of the footage may seem to be simply childrens' birthday parties and Christmas celebrations, you can find invaluable glimpses of the times in the rest.

If your community has a local television station, consider obtaining tapes of their local newscasts for your files. The tapes or films take a great deal of storage space but are a significant source of historical material. Many television stations otherwise throw out old newsfilm simply because they do not know what to do with it; if you have available storage space, you will certainly want to preserve it.

Records, of course, are primary source materials, and should be preserved at all costs. They may be tax records, court records and other legal material; they may be school or church records, business files, or even secretaries' books from organizations. You need them all.

Many states have laws specifying that when town, county or state records are microfilmed, the originals can either be offered to a historical society or must be destroyed. If you know that material is presently being filmed, get in touch with your state historical society to decide where the original records should go. Ideally, they should be preserved where there is a context of other research and reference materials, but if for reasons of space or other considerations the state historical society cannot handle them, some appropriate agency should take them over.

Churches and schools sometimes disband or unite with others, and their original records get lost in the shuffle. They are valuable historical source material. If you know the whereabouts of any old records now, acquire them; if you know that any churches or schools are presently about to change procedures, ask for all the record books for your collections.

Secretaries' books from organizations, ranging from the Chamber of Commerce to the Rotary Club to the Ladies' Tuesday Afternoon Study Club, can provide an astonishing amount of source material. Let each organization know that you are acquiring files for your historical society, and suggest that each turn over to you their old records. If, when you do acquire a particularly significant group of records, you could make much of it publicly, with newspaper stories and pictures, you would draw attention to your needs and purposes, and thereby stimulate other groups to hand over their records to you.

Businesses will be loathe to turn over any recent records to you, but you can talk to them about their correspondence and other material of, say 20 or 30 years ago, with the understanding that every few years they will give you another accumulation. The Union Pacific Railroad, for instance, recently donated to the Nebraska Historical Society all of its correspondence from 1860 to 1900—material that company obviously did not need for its current operations—which added a significant amount of source material to historians. If your community is dependent upon one or two industries, their old records could be invaluable to historians.

Recording historical information

In addition to locating and collecting historical information from available sources, there are certain kinds of material you must record yourself.

Cemetery inscriptions, for instance, are necessary notations. Every county has many small cemeteries which are now abandoned or vacated, and whose records have long since disappeared.

If there is an active local or state genealogy society, perhaps it has already compiled cemetery records and will share them with you; if not, you can assign a committee from your group to check the headstones, to copy down the information given there: names, birth dates, relationships, death dates, and other data. In some cases, the inscriptions may be so faint you will have to make rubbings or blow special preparations into the incisions to be able to read them.

If there is interest in organizing a genealogical society, you could suggest this as a beginning project for it, and help the new group begin its work. By working cooperatively with other agencies, all of you can benefit, sharing your finds and avoiding duplication of effort. Whoever takes the cemetery inscriptions, whether your group or another, should be sure that copies of the findings are located in several sites, both locally and in state genealogical and historical society libraries.

Recording cemetery data is an intriguing assignment for good-weather activity, and lends itself as a project for such volunteer groups as Boy Scouts or Girl Scouts, both of which can earn merit badges for historical work. The more groups, the more individuals you interest in historical study, the more support and understanding all of you will have in the community.

Historic sites of all kinds need to be verified and recorded. Try to identify the exact spots where something of importance happened, using all available plats, not only current but historic ones as well. Check old diaries and journals for landmark indications and interview oldtimers.

Use courthouse records (usually in the office of the Register of Deeds) to identify present and past owners of the land so you will know what particular persons or families to interview. In the West, check with the Bureau of Land Management about sites. The Office of Archeology and Historic Preservation of the National Park Service has two volumes, The National Register of Historic Places, 1972, and the National Register Supplement, 1974, which also provide source material on historic sites.

The detective work involved in authenticating precise locations is an assignment for patient, painstaking volunteers.

Record place names, particularly those of small communities which have dropped from sight or are dwindling in importance. A good place to begin is to study post office records, available through the National Archives, Washington, D.C. 20408—the Registers of Appointments of Postmasters. Duplicates of these records, available at small fees, give astonishing information about early-day communities; often the chatty reports tell how and why the names were given.

In addition to the material from the post office files, you will want to use plat maps to verify locations, and will want to interview old people in the area for other information.

Map-making

Historic map-making is a fascinating project. Secure a map of your area, with highways, rivers, railroads and other information marked on it. Maps may be available from the state highway department, from the U.S. Geological Survey or other sources. (A regular highway map, from the gas station, is usually cluttered with figures and symbols.) Have it enlarged to about 36 inches in width, so that it is big enough to work with. Mount it on a wall so that various members can work on it, and have them enter various sites of historic interest: "Smithville cemetery (abandoned), covered bridge, Indian encampment," whatever sites you feel are of historic interest. Make sure that each site is accurately located and marked, that it has been carefully researched, and that all dates and spellings are correct.

When you are positive that the map is 100% correct and that all possible historic sites have been listed, consider having the map printed on heavy paper and, if possible, in more than one color of ink.

The selling of maps can be a profitable venture over the years. Price individual copies so that you can recover the costs of making the plates and having the printing done within a reasonable length of time, but do not make them so expensive that people cannot afford them.

Community projects

There are many ways in which a historical society can work cooperatively with other organizations within the community to mutual advantage. Because these projects involve two separate groups of leaders, with different basic purposes, cooperative ventures require a great deal of planning and flexibility, but the results of these associated efforts are of benefit to all.

Speakers' bureau

One of the simplest projects to maintain, once it is established, is a speakers' bureau. Within any community there are a myriad of organizations requiring regular programs; civic clubs, such as Rotary, Kiwanis, Optimists and the like; women's study clubs of all kinds; professional groups such as accountants, secretaries, lawyers; and many others. If there is no list of them presently in existence, you can compile one from suggestions from your own members.

Develop a committed group within your organization of those of your members who can speak easily and well, and who have the time and inclination to work out speeches on a variety of historical topics—all well researched and historically accurate, all interestingly presented. Perhaps you could divide the duties, having some personnel devoted to doing research and others to preparing and delivering the speeches from that material.

In late summer, or whenever the various organizations are planning programs for the new season, send a notice to each of them indicating that you have program material available as a service to them. Also indicate that your speakers are available to fill in whenever an emergency arises and the clubs need last-minute help.

In the beginning, you will need to compile a great deal of historical material: the history of the medical profession in the region, for instance; the role of women in the community in the past, social customs and entertainment; the development of music or drama within the area with examples of early-day presentations; a general program of the basic political history; many others. You may want to prepare speeches on seasonal activities: how children celebrated Halloween a century ago; or how athletics, particularly football, were organized; or the household jobs a woman did every spring a century ago. You can use all of the research material at hand for these speeches, with old newspapers probably providing the most colorful details for the little nuggets that add human interest.

Keep a voluminous file of all of the speeches; within a year or two, you will have enough material to supply any club, at a moment's notice, with a program on any subject. Your speakers' bureau will be limited only by the number of persons who want to give speeches!

Each speech should be no more than 30 minutes in length, and a brief bit of it, no more, can mention the historical society, so that members of the audience can learn how they may join.

School projects

Many schools have at least some study of the history of the state as part of the social studies curriculum. Because faculty members change from time to time, many of them come from other geographic areas and are unaware of facilities in their new community; they often do not know of the existence of a local historical society. It is up to you to introduce yourself to them, and to tell them of the services you may be able to provide them.

To be of help in schools, you will need to work closely with the teachers. Tell them what material you have in your local historical society, what resources you have available to them. Offer to help them with research, arrange tours. Many teachers welcome outside lecturers in the classroom to talk to the children about local history and how it fits into the context of the general history of the state. You may suggest such a program, but if the teacher is not receptive, do not demand the chance to give it.

If you are to serve as guest lecturer in a classroom, plan carefully with the teacher to see how the subject will fit into the syllabus; if the instructor has already given general information to the class, for instance, your topic should be specific. The teacher may give guidelines or ask for a definite subject. Use human interest stories for illustrations, selecting them according to the age of the audience; if your group is in elementary school, tell how children their age dressed and what sorts of games they played long ago; if the group is older, adjust the content of the speech to their level. For school presentations, always allow some time for questions and answers, for if you do a good job of speaking, you will arouse the interest of the youngsters and they will want to know more. Children are rarely as inhibited about asking questions as their adult counterparts. Make the most of the limited class time, for when the bell rings, your audience must go.

For advanced history students in high school, you could suggest presenting a program on how to do historical research, telling of the use of records, old newspapers, and all other resource materials. A good teaching procedure would be to present a hypothetical case and ask students what kinds of information they would seek and where they would look for it; from there, you can go into more sophisticated information about research. Invite the students to your historical library to see for themselves what materials you have available. Some teachers will take over from there, assigning papers from their students so that they can put into practice what they have learned in theory about historical research. Some schools will even give help in an intern program, allowing advanced students credit for helping in the historical society.

The section on tours in a later chapter tells how to plan historical excursions for students as well as for the public generally.

Another project which can be coordinated into a school curriculum is that of securing oral history. Have the teachers—or members of the historical society, if that works better—teach the students how to interview, using the general guidelines given in the Oral History chapter. Ask each one to get material from the oldest member in their family, their neighborhood or of their acquaintance, interviewing them about specific events of the past in the community: a blizzard or hurricane, a tornado, customs now forgotten, farming with horses, or any other topic that suggests itself. If the students do not have access to tape recorders, they may write the notes down in question-and-answer form. Ask the teacher if you may have copies of that material; it should be of some historic value for your files.

If you have been able to establish good rapport with faculty members and the administration of the local schools, there is no need to confine your service to the social studies department, for composition classes can also benefit from your help. If the English teachers are receptive, you could suggest essay topics.

Say that the anniversary of the chartering of your town or county is approaching. The teacher could assign as a topic a specific part of local history: when the railroad came in and how it developed, or how the utilities were developed in the community, or the growth of the schools, or celebrations of the past, or recreational programs in the community, or any of a score of suggestions. The list is without end; you could suggest to the teacher the subjects you have a great deal of source material for, and let her make assignments to the students. They should be specific—not as one sixth grade teacher assigned, "200 years of American History."

If the teachers accept the idea of essays on local topics, they can coordinate the project into their regular curriculum, teaching students how to do research, how to organize a paper, how to footnote it. The students will work closely with your society for their information, and hopefully some of them will develop a lifelong interest in history. The teachers may be willing to let you make Xerox copies of the best papers for your files.

From an educational point of view, teachers shun the practice of contests, for although one youngster wins, the others do not and are often so badly discouraged they are no longer interested in history or composition or other academic pursuits.

Senior citizens' projects

Senior citizens are often the persons most interested in local history, but often are unable to leave the nursing homes where they live. You need to take history to them.

Your historical society can provide speeches and programs for them, as outlined in the section on Speakers' Bureau.

And your group can organize gatherings and parties for them. For instance, you could have a story-telling contest about particular celebrations, storms, or specific events of the past. Tape-record the stories and do your best to keep the yarn-spinners on the subject; know in advance that most of the stories, particularly the later ones, will undoubtedly be larger-than-life-size. The yarns will have to be verified and edited later on, but you may have renewed an interest in old-time stories which may pay dividends later on when you interview the persons individually.

You can ask them about games they played as children on the school playground, for instance, and have them dictate the rules and purposes of the game; write them down or tape-record them, for you may never have another chance to collect this bit of Americana. Old-timers in groups can spark each others' memories—several people recollecting together can revive more social history than if it were obtained individually.

Fair booths

If your community has an annual county fair, charity benefit, or other similar activity, your historical society could consider having a booth or exhibit of some kind there. Since fairs attract patrons of all ages, a display can serve as a good means of publicizing your group and its functions.

What can you display there? Anything that will tell about your society and its relationship to the community, anything that will impel passersby to stop and look. You should have something big enough and dramatic enough that people can see your exhibit from a distance, and something detailed enough that when they walk over to look at it there is material enough to look at to justify their stopping.

You should take all necessary precautions to guarantee security of anything you exhibit at a fair; have material bolted to the walls or floors, or behind glass cases, or chained to the counter so that small items cannot be pilfered. Although it is a bother to have to take things home at night and bring them back the next morning, that procedure is sometimes necessary to make sure that easily portable items do not get lost.

Pictures, maps and old newspapers are eye-catchers when they are displayed in an interesting fashion. If you have a number of photographs which you need to have identified, have them mounted so that people can look at them at close range, and then have paper available for them to write down what the pictures are about and who is in them. You would label each picture and have a clipboard nearby with corresponding markings on sheets of paper, with sufficient space by each for a detailed listing of who and what are in the photograph. In fact, you could make the identification of photographs a contest, offering some sort of public recognition to the individual who is able to identify the greatest number of pictures.

Something with action is interesting. You could set up some pieces of kitchen equipment that are operable: a sausage-stuffer, or a churn, or a frame to cut homemade grease and lye soap. You could go through just enough of the operations of each piece of equipment that your audience could understand how each one works. The volunteers who man the display could wear replicas of garments of the period, with long aprons covering their calico dresses and muslin petticoats.

You will, of course, have facilities at your fair booth to enroll new members in your society.

The possibilities of exhibits at a fair are endless, and will depend upon your ingenuity, your imagination, and your desire to plan and work. Whether your display is simple or elaborate, it should be well done to show the public that your historical society is a first-class organization.

Movie showings

Almost every community has individuals who have taken home movies through the years. Often there are sequences showing parades, civic events, school activities, even day-to-day pursuits.

Collect these as you can; many families who took movies 30 to 40 years ago no longer have any interest in them and are glad to find a home for them.

Collecting movies poses many problems. One is size, for in the 1920s and 1930s most home-movie cameras used 16-mm film. Later on, people bought 8-mm movie cameras, and more recently Super 8. Films of different sizes are not interchangeable, cannot be spliced together, and require different projectors.

Much of the earliest film was nitrate-base, which disintegrates into powder with age, is explosive and a fire hazard. It cannot be shipped through the mail, and is a peril in your files. If you have any nitrate film, take it to your local photography shop and ask that someone there make arrangements to have it duplicated, with the originals destroyed later.

Some film, even though acetate-base, is so old and so brittle it cannot be shown with a projector. Splice it together as best you can and send it off to be duplicated before you attempt to thread it into a projector.

Collect what you can, and when you have enough to work with, edit it carefully, cutting out a large portion of the endless mother-and-the-kiddie shots, birthday parties, and Christmas celebrations which seem to be the content of a large part of amateur movies. Splice the remainder together into as long a movie show as you can—it should be at least 20 minutes of running time, more if possible. If you can possibly afford to have it duplicated immediately, do so; once original film is scratched, it is eternally scratched!

When people learn that you are looking for movie film, reels will turn up in unexpected places—in attics, garages, trunks, in the possession of people who have long ago moved from the community. Few people ever consider that home movies are historical source material—but once they see priceless footage of Model T automobiles slewing around in the mud, or lugwheeled tractors in the harvest field, or little boys in knickerbockers playing marbles or scooting a scooter, they will remember what they have at home.

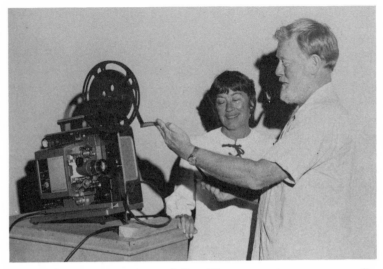

Amateur movies of activities of 40 or 50 years ago in your community can provide magnificent looks at social history, but the films need careful and drastic editing. If the old.film is brittle, it will have to be duplicated before you can work with it.

The editing of movies is a tedious, time-consuming affair, for you often must run through hundreds of feet of film to find a sequence that really shows how people lived back when. But the good movies are worth the effort for they are graphic, telling the story far better than any other medium can.

At first you can rely upon a borrowed projector, but if you plan an extensive movie program, you will need to have your own projector, an editor to simplify the editing process, and other technical equipment. Movies can become costly, for the duplication of film is expensive and must be done by professional laboratories. Some of your costs you can recover by charging a small admission fee—your audiences will be large. Other costs can possibly be covered from donations.

A movie project is one of the most exciting, most appealing presentations possible for local history; it is worth investigating.

OTHER HELP AVAILABLE

AASLH Technical Leaflet 36, *Filing Photographs.*

AASLH Technical Leaflet 18, *Historical Society Records: Guidelines for a Protection Program.*

AASLH Technical Leaflet 9, *Cemetery Transcribing.*

Oral History

Oral history is the unwritten, unpublished information that heretofore has been only in the minds of individuals. Oral history is what people say about what events have taken place. Oral history provides colorful, detailed information, usually supplementing other data, although in some cases the only knowledge about certain happenings is in the memories of individuals.

In primitive societies with no written language, all of the knowledge and lore of the past was handed down from one generation to the next by the recitation of legends. Much of our knowledge of American Indian history, for instance, comes from the oral tradition; stories were memorized by each succeeding generation.

Other cultures, not accustomed to relying on memory, have tended to overlook the "stories of the old men" as historical sources, concentrating instead on written records, journals, newspaper accounts. Within the past generation, however, as people use the telephone more and the written letter or diary or journal less, oral history has become more important to historians. Oral history brings a certain flavor and quality to words and ideas that the written word cannot convey.

With the development of magnetic tape and easy-to-use tape recorders, oral history programs have been established by many historical groups and are in the process of being refined to a science. Many persons "intend" to write memoirs but never get around to them, but they will talk about what has happened in the past; getting that information in permanent form, through the use of tape recordings, is a significant historical activity.

Most local historical societies utilize oral history in the form of interviewing old-timers in the community about their recollections of early days, often fleshing out dry records with lively, personal memoirs, sometimes finding out why some things happened and others did not, discovering cause-and-effect relationships, and occasionally capturing on tape the only information about long-ago activities.

To establish an effective oral history program, you need three basic tools. You need first to identify the people you will interview who are the most knowledgeable sources of information. You need to know how to interview them, what questions to ask, and how to proceed. And you need to know what equipment to use and how to use it.

Almost everybody in a community has some specific knowledge about something that nobody else has. The problem is to identify the people and what they know about.

Within your own historical society you can establish an oral history committee to make lists of specific persons with specific stories to tell: Mr. Jones, who is 88 and still sharp of mind, farmed for 65 years, using horse-drawn equipment and implements he tinkered together himself. He progressed through the development of tractors and more sophisticated machinery; he could tell us about the evolution of farming. Mrs. Brown, who is 85, burned tumble weed and corn cobs for fuel, made her own soap and fought prairie fires; she can tell us about everyday life on the farm in the old days. Dave Pawloski was involved in the bitter mine strike and can tell us about it from the miners' point of view. Harry Zilch was a rum-runner, moonshiner and bootlegger during prohibition days, and maybe he will tell us about that. Adam Smith was mayor when the underpass on Second Street was discussed but not built; perhaps he will give us some background information about that. Dr. Bones, who has been in practice since the horse-and-buggy days and performed kitchen-table surgery, can trace the changes in medical practice and tell of his own experiences.

The possibilities of oral interviews are endless. As soon as you get into the program, you will think of more and more persons who are obvious subjects for interviews. Naturally you will get the oldest ones first, before their minds or bodies go.

How do you go about interviewing? First get in touch with your subject, either by letter or by personal contact, advising him that you wish to talk with him about such-and-such a subject, explaining what your purposes are in obtaining information from him. Then set up an appointment so that your subject can be sifting his memory, checking his scrapbooks and talking with other people for information on the topic at hand.

While he is doing that, you will be preparing yourself. You will know in general what questions you will ask: who (and get exact names—not Aunt Helen, but Helen Jones, wife of Otto), what, when, where, why and how. In preparation for the interview, you check newspaper stories, legal documents, vital statistics, and other material so that you will know what kind of information you do not have but hope to get. If the nomenclature of the particular subject is likely to be alien to you, you even study what terms the person is likely to use. Ordinarily, however, you would have someone familiar with the topic do the interview.

Prepare a general outline, referring to it from time to time so that you will not stray too far from your purpose. In many cases, you will not have much of an idea when you start what kind of information you will find; it is sometimes easy, especially for a beginning interviewer, to become so absorbed in the interview that you lose sight of your intent. As you become more experienced, you will not need to rely on notes.

Arrive on time for your interview, plug in your equipment, and exchange a few pleasantries before you begin. Leave enough space on the tape that you can later go back and tape in the identification: name of interviewer, name of subject, date and place of the interview, and the general topic. If you put that in at the time of the interview, speaking into the microphone, the subject may be overcome with mike fright; many persons, especially older ones who have not grown up in the electronic age, are skittish about microphones.

Be relaxed and put your subject at ease, but not so much so that you are the star of the show. You are to get information from your subject; you are to ask the questions and if necessary steer him back to the topic, but you are only the instrument through which his information is obtained.

Begin asking questions, phrasing them in terms that will evoke memories. For instance, rather than asking "When was that?" in your interview about the epidemic, ask instead, "Was it in the middle of the summer? Before or after the Fourth of July?" Or if your subject is a farmer, ask, "Was it before the wheat harvest?" or "Was the corn picked?" Answers to these questions pin-point the exact time far better than if you had asked what month and date the event occurred. If you are interviewing an old-timer about an event far back in the past, you may ask, "What grade were you in?" or "Who was your teacher?" rather than the exact year; you can determine the year later.

Rather than describing a location as "across the road from Smith's house," try to get a legal description of the site: in town, the street names, the side of the street and the distance from an intersection; in a rural area, the township, range and section number. If the exact location is vital to your topic, take a map of the area and have your subject mark it, making the notation on tape to that effect.

You will want to take a note pad and pencil with you to check on the spelling of names, places and events, and to make other necessary notations which may be of use to you later.

If there are discrepancies between what the interviewee says and what you feel is really the truth, do not belabor the case; try to get an explanation, but do not antagonize your subject. Always remember that you are not the performer—your subject is, and it is his comments you want to tape.

Phrase your questions so that they cannot be answered by a simple yes or no, but will require explanations. If your subject seems to be reluctant to discuss something you really want to know about, rephrase the question in other terms: a good reporter, which is what you are, really, learns to go at topics from various different angles.

Avoid interviewing more than one person at a time; you can accomplish far more on a one-to-one basis, asking and answering questions with no outside interference. Spouses are often liabilities during an interview, the one not being interviewed sometimes disagreeing about specifics or the relevance of a particular comment. If you wish to interview both a man and his wife, do so separately; you can suggest in the second interview that Mr. Jones mentioned the fire in the livery barn and ask Mrs. Jones what she remembers about it, and get her version.

Many of your interviews will require more than one session, for you will not want to exhaust your subject; in fact, an hour, or an hour and a half at most, is the longest you will ever want to conduct a single interview. Make an appointment for the second session as you leave; in the meantime, your subject will probably remember many more details to tell you.

After you are completely finished with your interview of Mr. Jones, ask him to sign a simple document acknowledging that he has given this information willingly for educational and historical purposes. Sample wording of the form, typed on the historical society letterhead, could be as follows: "I hereby give and grant to the (Your-Name Historical Society) as a donation for such scholarly and educational purposes as the Society shall determine, the tape recordings and their contents listed below." The paper will be signed by the narrator and the interviewer, giving the date of the agreement and the subject of the tape or tapes.

As a local historical society, you will also interview persons who are prominent in business, political and community life; occasionally they may wish to put restrictions on the use of the information they supply you, saying that they do not wish to have the material published or made available to the public for a given number of years. Those restrictions are a headache; avoid them if you can, but if they are necessary to the obtaining of the material, accept them—and honor them, at all costs.

There are some legal problems concerned with material which you may secure through tape recording of oral history; two books which provide more detailed information are *Oral History for the Local Historical Society* by Willa K. Baum, published by the

American Association for State and Local History, and *Oral History Program Manual* by William W. Moss, published by Praeger Publishers.

What kind of equipment do you need for an oral history program?—the simplest, most foolproof equipment you can get!

You will want a tape recorder which is lightweight, easily portable, always operable, and one which will run with the last amount of technical motions. It should be usable on both regular electrical current and on batteries, for there may be occasions when you have no electricity readily available. When you use the tape recorder on battery power, be sure you have fresh batteries in the machine and a couple of spares in your pocket; when you go out on an interview to use the machine on electrical current, take an extension cord and possibly even an adapter socket with you.

For most purposes, a small, easily carried cassette-type tape recorder will serve your oral history program; it will record with less background noise if it has a separate microphone, rather than a built-in one.

Reel-to-reel tape recorders are necessary for occasions when you are recording musical performances or persons whose voices you want accurately recorded. Reel-type recorders have better fidelity; they are more expensive, however, and larger and heavier to carry. For most of your work, a cassette-type machine will serve your needs.

Buy your equipment locally from a reputable dealer, keep it simple, and make sure you know exactly how it operates; it should be uncomplicated enough that your various interviewers, even the nonmechanical types, can use it with a minimum of instruction. Most tape recorders require that two buttons, "record" and "play," be pushed before the machine records; be sure you understand exactly how to work it, and also how the microphone attaches to the machine.

Do not economize on tapes; buy first-quality stock which will give good reproduction of sound with a minimum of surface noise. The tapes should be either the 60- or 90-minute variety, 30 to 45 minutes on each side; you will not have 2-hour interviews, so that the 120-minute tapes are unnecessary. Save the boxes or plastic containers the tapes come in, for you will use those for storage.

When you set up your equipment, do not have the microphone and the tape recorder on the same table; you will record distressing noises from the machine itself. Set the microphone near your subject, on a scarf or handkerchief or some other deadening device to make sure there is no rattle or echo. The microphone should be in a relatively unobvious location, however, so that your subject is unaware of it as he talks. Once you have your equipment in place and in operation, don't fiddle with it, except to turn the cassette over when you have reached the end of the first side. Most cassette players will click when that time comes, and you should know from your watch about how much time has elapsed.

If your subject is a little ill at ease at first, or curious about the operation or recording of the tape recorder, when you set up for the interview you could record some idle chit-chat with him, then replay it to let him see how the machine works. That length of tape you could use later for your lead-in, the part on which you later record the name, date and topic of the interview.

As soon as you can, have your tape recording transcribed by one of your volunteers into a typed manuscript. The tape itself is more valuable than the typed copy, for it is a record of the person's voice; the nuances, the manner in which he answers your questions can give an insight into his personality that typed words cannot. However, a typed manuscript copy of the interview is a permanent record. Have at least three copies made: one for the state historical society, and two for your own files. Although tape cassettes are common now, it may be that within 25 or 50 years they will not be, and the means to play them back will have disappeared; if so, the tapes will then be useless. "Electrical transcriptions" were common in the years immediately prior to World War II; one high school class transcribed its members this way. But when it went to play back the wire recordings at its thirtieth reunion, it had to go to great lengths to locate an old wire recorder.

Depending on your subject, you may wish to give him a copy of the typescript to correct for factual data; tell him, however, that he is not to make a written essay of it, but merely to check names, places, or other specific information on it. Then make those corrections in your own transcript.

To store tape cassettes, place them in plastic containers before putting them into a cabinet; the tapes are magnetic and when they are in juxtaposition to metal, they can lose sonority.

What kinds of material can you secure from oral history? Loosely, whatever anyone wants to tell you! As you begin to interview subjects and find out what kinds of information you can gather from them, you will develop a wide-ranging program of oral history. No two interviews will be alike, and you will gain proficiency in interviewing with each succeeding session. With some of your interviews, you may want a follow-up to garner even more information than you were able to collect at first.

If you can afford an expensive tape recorder which gives a faithful reproduction of the voice, fine. If all you have is some junior high student's inexpensive tape recorder, use that; something is better than nothing.

Site-Marking

The permanent marking of historic sites is one of the most important functions of a local historical society—and one of the most frustrating as well. In the first spurt of enthusiasm, your society may rush out intending to mark practically every corner of town, every section of land.

But hold off, start at the beginning.

What do you mark? Look at your own history with an objective eye, and determine what really are the most significant historical events of the area. It does not always follow that the oldest is the most important, although you will probably include some of the "firsts"—site of the first house, first church, first school, for instance.

Then with a calm, collected committee, you will list the sites in order of priority. All things being equal—but they often aren't—you will install a marker at the most significant site first, then those of lesser significance, and so on down your priority list.

Having decided what to mark, you must then determine where and how to mark the site, and what to have on the legend. Markers are permanent; that is why you install them. The marker, and its legend, will presumably be there for eternity. Do not make a mistake that will last that long. Anything pertaining to a permanent marker must be not less than 100% accurate!

FALLING WATER AND
EARLY INDUSTRY

On these headwaters of the Blackwater River, 19th century industry flourished. The stream which begins here through its first few miles once powered the New London Scythe Company, a shingle mill, a saw mill, a grist mill, a woolen mill, a tannery, and other small industries. Upon such foundations modern American business and technology began.

Here is a good example of an aluminum historical marker made with heavy duty material, built to last. The wording is concise and all the most important information is included.

The National Register of Historic Places, 1972, and the Supplement, 1974, containing 7,000 entries arranged by state and county, may possibly provide assistance; perhaps your sites are already listed there. The books are available from the Superintendent of Documents, Government Printing Office, Washington, D.C. 20402.

Once you have decided which site is of first priority, begin studying all available records to make sure you have located the exact geographic spot. Whether or not you place the marker there is not important; you must know the precise location of, for instance, the Pony Express Station, if that is what you are marking. If for any reason you cannot place the marker there, you will want to know how many feet east of the sign the site was.

Use all available journals, plats, maps and other printed material; study old diaries to see if any natural landmarks are mentioned and if any distances are given. Old-timers in the area can sometimes give information which will provide valuable clues. Members of reputable metal detectors' clubs, working closely with landowners, historical society personnel and within the confines of state and federal laws, can sometimes find nails, shell casings, buttons or other metal artifacts under the topsoil which will help establish a precise location; metal detectors should not be allowed access to any historic spot, however, without close supervision.

The next order of business is what kind of marker you will install. Aluminum ones provide the most opportunity for wording; in addition, most state historical societies can provide some financial assistance with aluminum markers. But you may wish to have a granite or stone marker. Or, in some cases, molded resinous markers which have been proved durable to the elements; these, presumably, will not last as long as either stone or aluminum. Whatever you choose should be durable, able to withstand the elements and the ravages of vandals, and it should be something you can afford.

What do you write? The writing of legends is difficult because you want to tell a detailed, complete story in a very limited number of words. Some groups have spent months, perhaps more than a year, agonizing over a single legend, each word of it assuming tremendous importance. If you have a simple granite marker with just the name and date on it, you have fewer problems—but the people who see the marker will not have much of an idea about what its significance is. Work on the legend with earnestness, choosing the most striking information and finding single words that will take the place of several.

What are the legal considerations? Presumably before you began tramping over somebody else's property, you had permission to be there. But if the marker is not located on the exact site indicated in the marker text, you do not need to secure permission of the owner of the site to place a marker anywhere.

But where you do install the marker itself, you must secure a right-of-way from the landowner; after all, it is his land you wish to place something on permanently. If you wish the marker to be alongside a highway, you must negotiate with various governmental agencies, including the state Department of Roads. If you do not have an attorney among your members, hire one to handle these particular legal matters. He will be able to save you from possible difficulties later on.

Another consideration is the maintenance of the marker. Who will see that the weeds are cut near it? The marker pushed back in place if it is knocked askew? Determine who will maintain the marker before you begin mixing the concrete to set it.

How do you finance your marker? If it is one which has appeal to a specific group of people, ask them for contributions earmarked for that project. For instance, if it is a pioneer cemetery, ask surviving members of families buried there if they will help. Or if it is the site of the first factory in town, or a brickyard or forge, perhaps the Chamber of Commerce or members of an industrial group will help.

If you plan an extensive program of site-marking, budget what you can from your general treasury, and when you are not using

Unveiling a marker can be a dramatic event. Had this been an aluminum-type marker, the legend would have described what Liberal Hall was and its significance to the community. The speaker at left told the story, however, and his manuscript is now part of the local historical society's archives.

that amount put it into a savings account or certificates of deposit so that it will draw interest.

How can you cut some costs? If an old building in your community is being torn down, sometimes it is possible to salvage granite foundation stones or other material suitable for markers. Check with any wrecking crews in the area to see what they have scheduled, and whether it would be possible for you to salvage any material. Where will you store the stones? How will you transport them? Have you a member who owns a large, heavily constructed warehouse with some extra room? And one who owns a boom?

If you use stones as markers, you can have them cut during the off-season, usually winter. Many stonecutters—monument men—will work for more reasonable fees when they are not otherwise occupied. If you do not set an exact deadline but allow them to work at their own pace, you can sometimes get a more favorable rate from them.

When it is time to install the marker, you often can secure the volunteer services of Boy Scouts or other youth groups, who earn merit badges for historical work. They can help dig trenches, put together framing, mix and pour concrete, and even in some cases trowel it. They can help jimmy the marker—a few boys if it's an aluminum one, many if it's a granite one—to the proper location on the concrete foundation. One or two historians supervising a troop of Boy Scouts can accomplish a great deal when it's time to install a marker.

After the marker is installed, you will hold an elaborate unveiling ceremony, with appropriate city and county officials present, and perhaps music, with a speaker giving an appropriate brief speech about the importance of this site to the county, state and nation; you will have a gala time. It will take much planning, but it will be worth it.

OTHER HELP AVAILABLE

AASLH Technical Leaflet 32, *Historic Site Interpretation*.

Tours

Tours show history, geography, and cause-and-effect relationships, and all sorts of other things. Tours are picnics—for everybody except those who are in charge of them. Tours are a great means of getting many people involved in an easy, effortless study of their own history.

Planning a tour, a smooth running, happy tour, takes about a year of thoughtful, careful attention to details, historical as well as otherwise. A well-run tour is a delight; a sloppy one, a fiasco. The difference is in the planning.

Your tours will be in busses, rather than in automobile caravans. If you have a long string of cars, one in the middle always gets lost, with the result that the ones following him are lost, too. There are problems of parking, problems of dust if it is a tour along byroads. Passengers in automobiles cannot have the advantage of hearing the tour guide, and have no idea why they have come to this site. And also they miss the camaraderie of the bus ride itself.

If you have persons coming from a long distance for the tour, have them meet at a central location, park their cars there, and board the busses, returning by bus to the parking lot afterward.

Area tour, by chartered busses

Where do you want to tour? How do you establish an itinerary?

As soon as you decide what particular area you want to cover on your tour, get a large-scale map, preferably one which shows all roads, especially back roads. Divide the area into townships, or similar small subdivisions, and assign members of the tour committee to find out all they can about them, one man to a small subdivision. (If you can have a native, or a resident, working on his own area, he will have the advantage of much knowledge already.) Each committee member should write down all of the possible stopping points in his area, and as much general historical knowledge of each point as he has at hand.

With the map of the whole area at hand, plot a possible itinerary, using as little back-tracking and zig-zagging as possible. Which are the points you can leave out most easily? Which are the most important places? Work out your itinerary on paper first.

After you have a reasonably good idea of where you will go, begin research for specific information about the sites: why was this place important, what happened here, to whom, and when? What has happened to the place—or the people—since?

Then, with as many committee members as you can gather together, drive that route in a car, clocking carefully the distance between the points and the time it takes to cover each segment. You will make many changes in your itinerary as a result of that first dry run, and you should make several more trips over that route to refine it further.

Even after you have the historical part of the itinerary settled, you have other matters to consider. Where will you have rest stops, with adequate toilet facilities available? (Plan on a toilet stop every 2 hours.) Which sites along the way will you merely look at from the bus, and which will be get-out-and-look stops? Every time you unload many people from a bus, you slow up a tour; make sure each get-out-and-look stop is worth the time it takes. Is there really enough to see there to justify the stop? You should, however, arrange your tour so that you have those get-out-and-look stops every 30 to 45 minutes, at particularly scenic spots.

Many of your tour participants will be photographers, amateur or otherwise. When you are planning your itinerary, have a camera buff along to help pick out the photogenic areas or other spots that photographers will be especially attracted to, and allow time in your schedule for camera stops. The photographers on the tour will be unhappy if they are not permitted to get off the bus; they will insist, and unscheduled stops will upset your overall plan unless you have made allowances for flexibility.

Consider, too, the time of year. Tours along a stream or in a wooded area are often most effective in the fall, when the leaves are changing color; tours in orchard country are prettiest in the spring when the trees are in blossom. Weather, too, is important; do not schedule tours at times when you are reasonably sure the weather will be damp and unpleasant.

One beauty of tours is that they are usually on intriguing little back roads that most people seldom see, or even know about. Often tour participants include people who ordinarily don't care at all about history, but who enjoy the ride—and then find themselves involved in history in spite of themselves.

If it is an all-day tour—and that means 6 or 7 hours, no more—make arrangements for lunches. You can either have box lunches provided by a caterer, or you can have each tour participant bring his own sack lunch. Arrange a picnic-type stop at noontime at an attractive spot—and be sure restroom facilities are available, and adequate.

You'll also need a bad-weather alternative, just in case: a village hall, a country barn, or some other covered area to protect you from a pounding rainstorm. Make those arrangements in advance, so that you are not caught short.

How do you get busses? In most communities there are facilities for chartering busses for special tours. Can you secure them with public address systems? If not, then make arrangements for loudspeakers; your tour guides will need to be heard at the back of the bus, over the sound of the motor. If your society does not own a public address system, make arrangements to rent one for each bus on your tour. Make sure that passengers are insured by the bus company; if not, take out short-term insurance yourself.

In some geographic areas, where regular commercial busses

are not readily accessible, school busses may be—at standard mileage rates, including dead-head fees—if it is a weekend or some other time that the busses are not in normal operation. Make your inquiries and negotiations with the superintendent of the school and members of the school board involved. School busses usually have wide windows, no overhead racks to bang heads on, and no arm rests to hinder getting out of the bus. The drivers are accustomed to traveling those back roads, are thoroughly familiar with every curve, every hill; and if there has been a recent rain, know whether the roads are negotiable, for they drive them every day. Since those drivers are residents of the area, they usually have more interest in the tours than regular, commercial bus drivers do, and occasionally can add a nugget or two of knowledge. Upholstery and springs are often minimal, however, so that the other advantages of school busses are lost in a long, long trip over bumpy roads. When you use school busses, make sure you check on insurance; sometimes the bus and its occupants are covered, whether they are school related or not, but usually they are not. Do not EVER consider a tour without making sure the bus and passengers are adequately insured.

What about tour guides? On each bus, you will need a lecture guide, one of your members who has prepared a great deal of factual information, as well as human interest stories about each of the sites along the tour and about the area generally. The guide should not read the material, but should be able to deliver it in an easy, informal style, and should be able to answer any questions passengers may ask. Let the tour participants add information, too; sometimes they are familiar with the area themselves and can relate some historic lore. Without a well-qualified guide, the tour could be just any bus trip; with a guide, it is a historic experience.

Tour booklets make a tour memorable, for with well-prepared material, tour members can relive the tour every time they read it. Ideally, every tour participant is given a booklet or folder which contains a map of the area with the itinerary marked with a Magic Marker; a detailed listing of the itinerary and the historical and geographic points of interest along the way; copies of

All ages and sizes, including a state senator and a visitor from Germany, were represented on this all-day tour on a chartered schoolbus of historic areas in Adams county, Nebraska. The last stop was to a famed peony garden, where tour participants were allowed to pick flowers to take home.

stories of colorful legends about the sites; and other pertinent material you can supply. The material can be mimeographed, Xeroxed or printed; it should be detailed, accurate, and interestingly written.

An elegant touch is to label each folder with the name of the individual tour participant. (Saves arguments on the busses at the end of the trip, too.)

Another one is to have a name tag for each tour participant, an easy means of getting acquainted. (These are often supplied without charge by the Chamber of Commerce.) Be sure the names are printed in large letters with a black magic marker; a typewriter doesn't have type large enough to see at a distance. Name tags lose their effectiveness if you have to get close to a person and peer at his label before you speak to him.

The tour guide or person responsible on each bus may also

want to have a totebag of extra equipment for the comfort of passengers. If the air outside the bus is cooler than that inside, or if the air is humid, so that the windows possibly will steam over, have a roll of paper toweling to wipe them off. Sometimes it's useful, too, to have a box of tissues, a tin of aspirin, and even a few Band-Aids, just in case.

To determine the cost of a tour, add all of your costs—the charter for the bus, meal costs (if any), printing and mimeographing booklets, tickets, name tags (if you have to buy them), any entrance fees, public address system rental—and gear the cost of the individual tickets to 60% capacity of the bus. You will not conduct a tour for a smaller number than that, and you want to be sure you recover all of your costs from the tour.

You will take reservations in advance, including names of the tour participants (so that you can label the tour booklets and make out name tags) and the money, to assure that you won't be left with a half-empty bus.

If you have 100% capacity on the bus, you will make a little profit from the tour. Do not, however, consider tours as money-making projects; they are a historic function. If you do make a small profit, fine, but don't count on it. It is better to pare your costs to the lowest figure possible, to have repeat business and to generate interest in history.

Tours can be among the most exciting historic activities you sponsor. Use lavish publicity, through all possible means, to create enthusiasm for them.

Alternatives

In some areas, tours by bus are not practicable, but one-site tours are. Participants gather, using their own means of transportation, to visit a particular area as a group, with guides directing them at the site. This kind of expedition is particularly workable for an Indian site or a reconstructed fort, or any place where the area enroute to the major site is not particularly historic or scenic, the distances are great, and the tour participants would be coming from many different communities. The tour is the inspection of the site itself, not the means of getting there.

It is possible, too, to join forces with other adjoining local historical societies or the state historical society for longer tours outside the immediate region. Whether it is a half-day tour or one of several days, the same careful planning and attention to detail are essential for a well-run excursion. An overnight tour requires block-booking of hotel or motel space, arrangements for mass feeding, and usually some sort of brief historical lecture or slide presentation in the evening; you can work with a local travel agent for specific help.

Walking tours, town tours

In many ways, walking tours of historic buildings and homes in the community are more difficult to plan than a long bus tour because participants are scattered all over, not confined into a manageable group.

You will need to spend a great deal of time planning what

Walking tours of architecturally important buildings or historic neighborhoods are always popular. Researching the various details and the significance of each site takes much time, but the resulting benefits make it well worth the effort.

buildings will be open on the tour, making necessary arrangements with the owners, and then establishing the traffic flow. Either have general guides to take people from site A to site B to site C, or else have carefully marked maps so that tour participants follow the same pattern. Keep the tour route consistent, so that people go from one site to another in a sequential pattern, not milling around in confusion.

Make sure owners' private possessions are out of the way, and that a supervisor or guard is in each room to protect against light-fingered tour participants.

Guides should be situated in each building to tell what it is and why it is significant. Tour booklets are not as important for a walking tour as they are for a bus tour, but they can provide much historic information that the participants can enjoy re-reading long after the tour is over. If there are large groups in a tour, milling around in an entranceway to a home, for instance, some people cannot hear; if they have tour booklets which they can read later, they will have a better knowledge of what they have seen.

In some communities, combinations of walking tours and bus tours have been handled with ease. The walking tour is confined to an area only a few blocks square; the busses are at a designated spot, and they then take passengers to sites at a distance. Follow the suggestions given for both kinds of tours if you plan a combination of both.

OTHER HELP AVAILABLE

AASLH Technical Leaflet 25, *Planning Tours.*

Establishing a Historical Library

After you have begun to collect historical material, you will need to gather it together in a historical library. You must arrange adequate security for your files of photographs and historical material and you must arrange to make your material available to researchers who wish to use it, keeping it intact all the while.

The simplest and most economical way to establish a historical library is, of course, to make use of already existing facilities. But there are pitfalls. You must make sure that your material remains intact and under your supervision at all times, and that it is not merged into other collections.

If you move your material into a public library, for instance, be sure that it is in a completely separate part of the building and at no time is considered part of the general library material. Title to it remains in the name of the historical society. You will want to make entries in the library catalog to indicate that the materials are in the historical society; this procedure helps patrons locate the information and therefore benefits both the library and the historical society. Those who work in the circulating library should not be allowed access to your historical information; only responsible representatives of your own society should be allowed to supervise it. At no time should any of your historical data be removed from the room.

The prime purpose of a circulating library is to get material into circulation, with books and magazines and other materials being checked out and taken from the premises to be read and utilized elsewhere. The mark of a good circulating library is the amount of its material not on the shelves but in use. Libraries are viable, constantly changing, with new books being added to collections and old, unused ones being removed.

Historical material is different; it is gathered together painstakingly, it is irreplaceable, and it should not be allowed to circulate generally. A historical library is one that hoards its material.

Any library is only as good as its system of cataloguing. Once information is put into file folders, it is lost forever unless you

A microfilm reader is essential if you plan to utilize microfilmed newspapers or other material. Most historical material is preserved on 35 mm roll film, but be sure to check what yours is before you invest in a reader; many readers can be converted to accommodate micro-fiche, a smaller-sized film which needs different holders and greater magnification. The roll of film on the machine pictured here holds about 3 months' worth of daily newspapers.

have an efficient system of retrieval, unless you know how to find it.

Your bibliographical lists will provide the first step toward historical cataloguing. Your indexes of material will be the second step. From then on, you will need to develop an efficient system of cataloguing and filing.

If you plan to establish a historical library, you will need professional help in the beginning. The state historical society may be able to provide personnel to help train your volunteers to establish a filing system; the American Association for State and Local History has consultative services which also supply technical expertise. You are looking for someone with historical training, rather than one trained in library science; ideally, your cataloguer will be a recent graduate student in history who is accustomed to doing serious research and therefore familiar with the usual cataloguing procedures. Ask for professional help before you begin filing your material, so that from the start all of your cataloguing will be done efficiently and properly. Indexing, cataloguing and filing of historical material is a function for historians, not librarians.

The volunteers who man your library should be trained carefully before they begin their work, so that the same patterns, the same systems of cataloguing and filing are utilized, and there is uniformity. The best means of guaranteeing a single procedural system is to work out a manual of instructions which everyone follows.

OTHER HELP AVAILABLE

AASLH Technical Leaflet 27, *The Library*.
AASLH Technical Leaflet 57, *Cataloguing Photographs*.

Preservation of Buildings

For many generations, the idea of preserving old buildings was alien to the American philosophy of "newer is better." With the whole country to spread out onto, as townspeople needed bigger buildings for expanding functions, they went on out from the center of town, leaving the older structures behind to crumble as they would. In the past hundred years, however, builders have gone back to those crumbling areas and demolished the buildings to make use of the land, often to construct new glass-and-metal structures on it, justifying their actions by saying "the location is worth it."

Why preserve old buildings?

Only in recent decades have communities awakened to the fact that most of their old buildings are now gone, that the structures left represent only the past few decades, and that there is little still standing to remind them of an old and significant past. In many communities, only the threat of a bulldozer will push the town into the realization that it has a fine old historic structure that should be preserved, that this is the last of the buildings remaining of a particular era, and that the building represents part of the historic heritage of the community.

A town that has all of its buildings of the same architectural period often has a dull sameness to it—it lacks distinction. A town that has a mixture, a blend of the old and the new, is a challenging one, obviously looking ahead as well as to its heritage, building for the future on the contributions of past generations.

Almost every community has buildings which are still structurally sound, representative of architectural and historic eras, and which are threatening to become eye-sores from neglect and victims of the demolition squad. The voice of your local historical society is often the only one that will be raised against this; you must provide leadership for the entire community to understand and appreciate the value it has in its old buildings.

Preservation is different from restoration

At the outset, we must distinguish between two commonly used terms: *preservation and restoration.* Preservation is not the restoration of a building to its past functions with all furnishings intact. It is, instead, the conservation of the structure itself, the maintenance of its basic design and building materials. In generally accepted usage, preservation is keeping a building in an "as is" condition. Such an effort could be quite an undertaking, requiring massive supports for decaying walls and foundations or patching weak and damaged roofs. The preservation of old log cabins is a case in point, where architects spray or infuse the wood with chemicals to prevent further deterioration and stabilize its condition. *Restoration* is another step, the physical changing of a building to return it to an earlier time period. This process will be discussed in the following chapter. *Reconstruction* involves the rebuilding of a structure partly or wholly destroyed by the ravages of time. The Governor's Palace at Williamsburg is a well-known example of a careful reconstruction.

A useful and manageable project for the local historical society along these lines would be the encouragement of the community to preserve and adapt old buildings to functional modern purposes. This specialized kind of preservation is called *adaptive preservation* or *adaptive use*.

A fine old mansion can be used as a funeral home or an elegant

A successful community effort to preserve a landmark is always a source of pride and a boost to interest in local history. Note the flag over the tower.

restaurant; an old **railroad** station can be turned into a shop or a restaurant or even, as in one case, into a neighborhood drive-in bank facility; an old church can be turned into an office for a monument company, for instance, or a school; an old country schoolhouse can serve as an art gallery. An entire block of business warehouses can be used for offices, stores and small shops, perhaps far different from the original purposes of the buildings. Old rows of early-day flats can be turned into sophisticated apartments; old barns can become highly desirable residential quarters.

In the adaptive preservation of buildings, the emphasis may be on **saving** the appearance and authenticity of the exterior. The interior of the building need not follow the original historic period in decor and furnishings, and it usually does not. It will have the necessary **fluorescent** lighting, stainless steel and glass, plumbing fixtures and other appurtenances for the efficient conduct of the present-day business. The old building will be adapted to a new use, and although its interior will be new, its exterior will save the appearance of the original structure.

What can your historical society do?

What can your historical society do about preserving old buildings?

The first step is to determine what you have in the community, and then to decide what is worth saving.

You will have worked with the Chamber of Commerce and with key businessmen to let them know what you are doing, and to generate interest and financial support from them. When they realize that the preservation of old buildings and putting them to adaptive uses in the community can be an asset to the whole town, they may be agreeable to joining forces with you; in many cases, preserving old buildings and putting them to new use is a means of rejuvenating a downtown area that is decaying. In other cases, such work helps save a residential neighborhood that is beginning to deteriorate. The preservation of buildings is a community effort, and you should realize that your historical society may be merely the catalyst that sets the whole undertaking into motion. Your group will suggest, explain, interpret, stimulate enthusiasm and provide the moral support, even though the implementation of the job will probably be the responsibility of other groups. No matter who does the actual construction of the job, you ought to cooperate fully and provide all the help you possibly can.

To determine what you have in the community, you will need to call in an expert from the outside to make a survey; he or she will not be swayed by emotion but will be able to study the town objectively—homes, public buildings, factories, stores, railroad stations, bridges, all structures. An expert will be able to see what is underneath the redone store fronts to point out that under the marbleized glass facades, for instance, there are architectural treasures from the Victorian age.

The expert may charge $200 per day or more, and may require

two or three days to study your community to give you the professional judgment you want. How to locate such an expert? Your state historical society may have lists of architects who are qualified to evaluate historical architecture; a school of architecture may have suggestions, or a large-sized architectural firm may have persons on the staff who are qualified. In some areas of the country, there are architectural concerns which specialize in adapting old structures into new uses; the American Institute of Architects (AIA) may be able to provide you with lists. You will be surprised to discover how many professional architectural historians are available to study old buildings with an eye to preservation.

To prepare for the study, your historical society should make lists of old buildings to help your outside expert get started, and gather old photographs to show how the buildings looked in years past. It may be that buildings your members have completely overlooked have architectural details of distinction which have been covered up or so altered that you were unaware of them, or that other buildings which you thought were of no particular significance possess some rare qualities.

The expert may make a "windshield" survey at first, listing property that he considers worth saving, composing the list in the order of importance. He will tell how valuable buildings are from an architectural point of view, as well as from a historical one. He will also list areas which might become historical areas.

As soon as you have his report, you will want to make it public. You should see to it that the local newspaper publishes stories about it, with photographs; you will want to organize walking tours (see Chapter 8 for suggestions about tours) so that people can see the buildings as they are now and can learn of their past. You will work out slide presentations for community groups, such as Lions clubs and others to stimulate community support, and you will utilize radio and television media to help you publicize the report about your town and its treasures. Your community must be aware of what your historical society, and others, hope to do with it and for it.

A Victorian bank in Red Cloud, Nebraska, has been preserved and adapted for another use; it is the Willa Cather Pioneer Memorial and Educational Foundation Building. The red brick and sandstone building was in use as a bank during the time that Cather lived in the town so that the conversion of the building to another use is a logical one.

Volunteer laborers, working under close supervision of restoration specialists, repair the interior of the long-unused bank building which is now preserved for use as a museum.

The next step, after you have had the survey made and had it publicized, is to insure that the properties suggested for preservation will remain intact until they can be worked on. To this end, you should apply to get them listed in the National Register of Historic Places. The State Preservation Officer at your state historical society can help you with the name and address of the state agency you will work with for the listing and will be able to make suggestions about procedures to follow. See Appendix E for the criteria used for evaluation by the National Register, and a list of state historic preservation officers. It does take time to be accepted on the National Register, but the waiting period can be reduced if you do a very careful report and include all the necessary data. The time and effort are well spent, for the recognition afforded will provide status to the project, showing the public that the building is indeed worthy of being preserved. (If, on the other hand, it is not accepted for registry, then you may want to question whether to go ahead with the project of adaptive preservation; perhaps the effort could be better spent on another project.)

The job of preserving old buildings and adapting them to other uses is one that not all local historical societies want to undertake by themselves, simply because of the cost. But the encouragement of local historical societies is essential to stimulate others, whether they are business concerns preserving an old blacksmith shop or forge to serve as an art gallery or boutique; a manufacturing concern preserving the original factory to serve as its office building; a group of businessmen banding together to provide funds to preserve an old block of sturdy, granite business structures in the center of town; or a quasi-governmental agency formed to utilize city, county, and private funds to preserve a whole area of town.

Your society will provide photographs, sketches or woodcuts, newspaper clippings describing the building, and any other information from its archives which will help recreate the structure as it was historically, before false-fronts and dryrot set in. You will work with artists or architects who are trying to picture the building as it will look after preservation is achieved.

You will want to provide publicity of all kinds to make sure that everyone knows what is going on and its importance to the community; you will lend your society's name to endorse efforts toward preservation of buildings which in turn preserve the heritage of the town. As outsiders are sometimes listened to with more credence than those who live in town, your society should sponsor appearances of outside experts—historians, urban planners, architects—to encourage the acceptance of the project. Whatever needs to be done to stimulate public interest in the project, your society should do willingly.

If there are zoning requirements or other technical problems to be taken care of before the preserved building can be adapted to another use, your society will lend assistance.

And further, your society will recognize and honor the efforts of all in the community who foster the preservation of significant old buildings by awarding plaques and other tokens signifying your approval and endorsement of the undertaking. These plaques may be bronze or other metal markers which can be affixed to the building itself, giving public notice that the histori cal society approves the preservation; they may also include some small legend, saying "This building was the site of the first flourmill in the county, erected in 1819, abandoned in 1912, preserved in 1976." The plaque could also say, "This plaque awarded by the Smith Center Historical Society for the preservation of this building as a reminder of our heritage from the past," or some such legend.

Whether the preservation in your community is merely one building—a log cabin to serve as a knit shop—or an entire area, such as Larimer Square in Denver, or Historic Pensacola, or those in Pittsburgh or Keokuk—the role of your local historical society is essential and significant.

Restorations

Restoration is the returning of a historic house or building to its condition in a given period of time, the structure and all its furnishings all accurate historically. A restoration requires much research and careful attention to historical detail; the building itself becomes a museum.

If there are distinguished old buildings in your community which your historical society wishes to save, you must consider whether you wish to preserve them as buildings or restore them as museums. Adaptive preservation is the retaining of the structure to use for whatever purpose is economically feasible; the building itself is preserved but its function can be adapted to uses completely different from its original purpose, and its interior arrangement and furnishings can be far removed from the historical period it represents. Restoration is the bringing back of the building to its original purpose, the furnishings, structure and even landscaping being a faithful portrayal of the original.

Restoration is obviously the more costly of the two procedures, as well as more time- and energy-consuming. If you plan to restore a building, you must have a good reason for your action.

Why restore a building?

Perhaps the architectural style is particularly significant. It may be a splendid example of Frank Lloyd Wright's design, or a

This splendid old residence in Fremont, Nebraska, has been restored and is used now as a museum and the headquarters of the Dodge County Historical Society.

pre-Revolutionary salt-box home, or a residence especially typical of Victorian architecture, with leaded windows, balconies and turrets, fretwork furbelows and fancy wood turnings. It may be an illuminating example of ethnic heritage, a Sunday House of the German immigrants in Texas or a Swiss chalet of Ohio immigrants. Or it may be an ornate castle-like structure built by new industrial money in the early years of the twentieth century, such as the Bellingrath home in Alabama or Stan Hywet Hall in Akron. Other examples of homes restored because of their special architectural significance include Oakleigh in Mobile, Rosedown Plantation in St. Thomasville, Louisiana, and the Gitch home in Des Moines. All are restored to reflect their architectural period, with furnishings appropriate to that era and set in landscaping which also echoes the period. The restorations themselves are the museums.

Perhaps an important person lived there or an important event occurred there. Then the building can be restored as a documentary site, significant historically. The homes of Presidents of the United States are examples—Mount Vernon, home of George Washington, Monticello, home of Thomas Jefferson, and the Hermitage, home of Andrew Jackson, being perhaps the best-known. They have been restored to reflect the period in which Washington, Jefferson, and Jackson lived there. The boyhood homes of some other presidents have also been restored, those of Lyndon B. Johnson in Texas and Herbert C. Hoover in Iowa, for instance, reflect the years those presidents were youngsters living there, not the years of their adulthood. Insofar as possible, furniture and artifacts are the original ones used in those homes; where these have been impossible to find, the furnishings that have been acquired for them have been of the same general historic period and geographical area. Of course all additions in the restoration—furniture, lighting, wall coverings and the like, should be carefully documented through wills, inventories, public records and other sources.

Your community may have been the home of a significant inventor, industrialist, writer, or some other individual of national importance, and the building where he lived or worked may be one that your historical society would like to restore to commemorate his contributions to the country. Or perhaps an important historical event took place in your town—the signing of an Indian treaty, the first sawmill in the territory, the first commercial radio station in the country, the first forge west of the Rocky Mountains. These sites could be restored to the period in which those events took place.

Perhaps there are restorations that could be made in your community which would be typical of an era. The Bullfinch homes in Orfort, New Hampshire, illustrate a way of living in the Federal period; the restorations in Natchez, Mississippi, show antebellum living in the South; Mystic Seaport in Connecticut, demonstrates the whaling-ship era in New England; and Pioneer Village in Minden, Nebraska shows frontier life of a century ago. These are restorations which make it possible for this and future generations to picture vividly how past generations lived, worked, made their living, and spent their leisure time. Other restorations typical of an era include the Living Farm restorations which show farm life of several generations ago, and

Restoration can take many forms. The Stuhr Museum of the Prairie Pioneer has recreated a pioneer village of about 1890, moving onto the location old farm buildings and old store buildings, restoring them to their original condition. The dirt road and the wooden sidewalk help intensify the recreation.

the Shaker Village or other communal villages in various parts of the country. These restorations are sometimes clusters of buildings which recreate parts of villages; Old Sturbridge Village in Massachusetts, for example, is a carefully planned recreation of a typical early nineteenth-century New England town.

Other reasons for restorations could be that the buildings are part of a historic section or neighborhood; these restorations are often contiguous to others which have already been restored or preserved by other agencies. The aim here is to keep the charm and flavor of an older section intact, be it a residential area or a waterfront section. Then, too, there are buildings which have great local sentiment and for that reason are sufficiently important for your local historical society to consider restoring them to their original appearance.

You must have a logical reason for wanting to restore a building to its original purpose and appearance before you begin the laborious process of making it into a museum piece. Its status as an old building is not enough.

Administering a site

Having decided that your historical society does want to undertake the restoration process, you must be aware of the problems and pitfalls that may arise. In the early stages of your restoration, you will follow many of the steps suggested in Chapter 10 on Preservations, particularly in enlisting community support and in getting the building on the National Register of Historic Places. You will need professional help from architects, historians, and specialists in many fields to help you begin the actual process of reconstruction. As mentioned above, consult your state Preservation Officer for advice and lists of restoration architects. But before that, there are other, more mundane problems to consider.

How will you administer such a site? Does an organization already exist which will be in charge of it, a legal entity to control. it and assume responsibility for it? Who will make the decisions, supervise the operations, take care of the property? There must be a governing body of some sort to oversee the financing, the day-to-day operations, the planning and policy-making that such a proposition entails.

Where will the money come from for the restoration of the building, and more importantly, for its maintenance and daily operation? This includes not only the rebuilding of the elegant old Italian tile roof, which is a visible, more-or-less glamorous undertaking, but also the heating and lighting bills, the salary of the curator who is there to supervise and interpret the site, the wages of the man to plant the boxwood and keep the lawns mowed, and even the wages of the security staff which protects it against possible human predators. It is easy to acquire a building; in fact, many local historical societies have been offered buildings free of charge—and the public has not really understood why they sometimes would not accept them, being unaware that such buildings can become albatrosses. The expense comes after the building has been signed over to the society.

Who will maintain the building? Can you secure funds from the local government, from continuing grants from foundations, from outright gifts? There is little likelihood you will be able to maintain a restoration simply from admission charges. It takes more money than that to pay the janitor who sweeps and dusts and replaces lightbulbs, the seamstress who repairs the rips in the splitting old satin draperies, the multitudinous day-to-day operational expenses.

Many persons are eager to give property to local historical societies for restoration, and even an initial amount to help get the restoration in progress. There is glory in that, but there is little in providing funds for the unseen, but even more important daily operational and maintenance costs.

If your local historical society is offered a building for restoration, and if after careful, thoughtful consideration decides to accept it, you must organize a governing board for it. You will need businessmen and administrators, as well as historians, to establish policy, set down rules, determine the purpose and extent of the restoration.

One of the first considerations for the board will be to establish the period of time of the restoration. If the building is one that commemorates a particular individual—the home of Willa Cather, for instance—then determine what particular era you wish for the restoration: will it be of her early days in the pioneer period of the 1870s, for instance, or will it be of a later period in her life, during the 1920s? If it is an old bank building, will you restore it to the condition it was in when it began in 1900, or when it was robbed in a spectacular cops-and-robbers event in 1935? The older the building, the more purposes it filled in its lifetime, the more difficult the decision will be as to the exact period for the restoration. But the period must be established by the governing board and must be written down in the minutes of the governing body's proceeedings.

The second task of the board will be to have a study made of the property by an architectural historian or other trained specialist, preferably an expert from outside the community. (See Chapter 10, on Preservations, for suggestions about how to locate the expert you will need.) The first survey may be made by a generalist, one who does not specialize in any specific kind of restorations but who will help you with the Master Plan.

Master Plan to evaluate whole operation

The Master Plan is the key to the whole restoration project. It should include an evaluation of the soundness of the building—has dry rot set in, are there termites, are the load-bearing beams sound or must they be reenforced with steel, does the mortar need repointing, is the roof sound?

It will include a determination of what alterations have been made to the property since the time of its greatest historic interest. Has a new wing or ell been added which will need to be removed? Has an old veranda been closed in, or worse yet, removed? Have the original windows been blocked in or enlarged? All of the changes that have been made in the structure over the years which affect the authenticity of the building will be noted so that you will know what renovations to make before getting back to the original design of the building.

The Master Plan should include a determination, with the advice of the expert you have hired, of the exact period to which you wish to restore the building. Your governing body will have discussed the matter at some length, but perhaps the architectural historian whom you engage for professional help will be able to suggest some possibilities that had not occurred to you.

The Master Plan specifically for the site should include such nonhistoric but essential items as parking facilities, visitor traffic flow pattern, restrooms, office area, maintenance service area. You must make provision for these services before you can begin to think about the actual restoration of the site. To help you develop the Master Plan, you will probably need the advice of a number of experts who have had enough experience with other restorations to realize what is involved. At times, it may seem to you that the historic renovation of the old building is the least important problem, so involved is the planning for the auxiliary areas.

As soon as you have the Master Plan sketched out, you will need to list priorities. What is the most important job to tackle

Even in a restored building, you need space for essential services; this is the office of the Louis E. May Museum in Fremont, Nebraska. Other space has been allocated to the gift shop, whose profits help with some operational costs.

first? second? third? How long will it take you to accomplish each step of your plan? In most cases it will take several years before the restoration is as you imagine it now.

Finally, the expert who is helping you with the plans will help you locate special builders and other construction personnel who will be able to handle specific details. Not every carpenter can repair the plaster mouldings in the ceiling nor the patterned tin. You will need to know where to find specialized workers for many of the esoteric details.

With your Master Plan in hand, the blueprint of what the site will look like when the restoration is complete, and with a rough idea of the costs of such a restoration, you should meet with your board to determine how far you will be able to go and how fast you can get there. You will have to plan your goals for the next several years, and the fund drives that will be necessary before you can go ahead. You need to remember that insofar as the public is concerned, all you are doing is restoring an old building; you should plan to intersperse the essential but nonexciting work with other, highly visible, dramatic improvements. A parking lot is necessary but not particularly stimulating to the public imagination; the locating, cleaning and installing of old millstones in the sawmill is far more intriguing. You will use all the psychological ploys at your command, making use of as much publicity as possible for the dramatic aspects of the restoration. For your fund drives, you will want to make use of suggestions in Chapter 3 on Financing, and all of the expertise your board of businessmen and administrators can summon; your experts will be able to put forth other ideas from previous restorations they have worked with.

Interpretation of the site

The last step in the restoration process is the interpretation of the site. Why have you restored this building? What does it show? Why is it important? As soon as you have enough of the restoration accomplished to begin admitting visitors, you must work out a means of telling the story in an understandable way. The restoration itself is only as significant as its explanation or interpretation; otherwise it is still just an old building. Does the building show the life of an important person. the evoiution of a particular industry? a way of living of an era?

To interpret a site, you will need to have exhibits set up in a logical pattern, you will need to have guides trained to explain it, and you will need to have printed brochures to fill in the gaps. The interpretation of the site is its reason for being.

Restorations are fascinating projects for a local historical society, and can become focal points for enlisting the aid of the entire community. They require detailed, careful historical research to make sure they are accurate. They need precise attention to administrative detail and overall, long-range planning. They call for imaginative interpretation so that their purpose is discernible and valid. Restorations call for energy, constant planning, and large sums of money. Before your local historical society undertakes to restore an old building that somebody has given you, consider carefully your responsibility for the varied processes necessary for that restoration.

OTHER HELP AVAILABLE

The Restoration Manual, by Orin M. Bullock, Jr., available from American Association for State and Local History.

AASLH Technical Leaflet 74, *Log Cabin Restoration: Guidelines for the Historical Society.*

AASLH Technical Leaflet 76, *Rescuing Historic Wallpaper: Identification, Preservation, Restoration.*

AASLH Technical Leaflet 77, *Wood Deterioration: Causes, Detection and Prevention.*

AASLH Technical Leaflet 80, *Historic Landscapes and Gardens: Procedures for Restoration.*

AASLH Technical Leaflet 17, *Furnishing Historic Houses.*

AASLH Technical Leaflet 15, *Paint Color Research.*

AASLH Technical Leaflet 48, *Nail Chronology.*

AASLH Technical Leaflet 67, *Pre-restoration Preparation.*

Protecting Our Heritage: A Discourse on Fire Protection and Prevention in Historic Buildings and Landmarks, Joseph Jenkins, editor, available from American Association for State and Local History.

Interpretation of Historic Sites, by William T. Alderson and Shirley P. Low, American Association for State and Local History.

Museums

A local museum is usually the outgrowth of individual collections of objects and artifacts, with many others being added to that as the museum program gains momentum. It is relatively easy to start a museum—but the maintenance of one is complicated and expensive. Consider the costs carefully before you begin.

Where will your museum be?

Will it be in an old building which has been restored? An old bank, an old store, an old railroad station, a fine old home? (And if so, what about restoration costs, even before you've moved in your first exhibit?)

Will it be accessible to drop-in traffic, in the main part of town? Will parking space be available?

How will it be maintained? Who will pay for the costs of utilities, repairs, insurance and security?

How will it be staffed? Records kept? Exhibits prepared, labeling done, preservation and restoration of materials accomplished?

The costs of starting and keeping a museum are so great that you must consider them carefully before you make up your mind, as a local historical society, that you can assume the responsibility for one.

Financing can come from many different sources. For capital

construction, you may be able to secure support from the city or the county, from revenue-sharing funds (if they continue to be available), from benevolent individuals, and from businesses. There are seldom federal funds available for capital construction.

For maintenance, you may secure a city or a county mill-levy. Added funds can come from entrance fees, giftshop profits, and membership fees, but all of those smaller monies added up will not be sufficient to maintain a museum.

Museums tend to be the attics of the community. What do you want in yours, what will you accept, and what do you not want? Do you plan to concentrate on specific subjects, specific periods of time, a specific geographic area? You must decide in the beginning what you want, or you will soon look like a garage sale. Many local museums, long organized, are now having to decide what they really want to be, and are having to weed out material that has been donated to them, and accepted by them in good faith in years past. Eliminating material after it has been accepted can sometimes cause ill-feeling among the patrons.

At the time you accept donations, be careful what commitments are made to the donor in terms of use and display, so that the donor understands what has not been promised. When you accept those donations, have proper legal forms for all parties involved to sign, acknowledging receipt of them so that descendants cannot challenge the validity of a donation.

After you have financing arranged and the building acquired, you begin the job of moving in, of arranging your materials, of attending to the purpose of the museum. What is that purpose? It is to interpret the past through the display of artifacts, to tell the story of what happened by exhibiting relics, objects, other materials in context.

A museum display should be an educational experience. Just as one picture is worth a thousand words, so one three-dimensional object is worth a thousand pictures.

If you have many kitchen articles of a particular period, for instance, display them together, and through the use of well-done labels, tell what each item was used for. As a backdrop for the exhibit, you could even use a greatly enlarged photograph of

This is an excellent museum exhibit, combining well-labeled maps, documents, historic paintings, and artifacts to see and to touch. It tells a complete story.

a kitchen of the period to show the range, the table, the working space, so that the function of the utensils you display is obvious. A kitchen range poker by itself is a mystery unless the viewer knows what it was used for; when it is exhibited in a logical place in relationship with other kitchen equipment, it is part of the story.

Just because Mrs. So-and-so gave you many things, do not feel that you must keep them all together in one exhibit, labeled "Mrs. So-and-so." They may be far more effective if the items are separated and grouped according to function or in some other logical arrangement. Through the documents you both signed when she donated the material to your museum, you will have made your position clear.

Each display should teach. It should not be a hodgepodge collection of curiosities and relics, and it certainly need not include every single object the museum possesses. Arranging a display is far different from packing a suitcase, or a display cabinet; you should not say, "Ah, here's a corner over here about the right size—I'll put this vase here!" Instead, you should consider, "Where can this vase add effectively to the total story we are trying to tell?"

If you have many lace fans, for instance, consider what you want them to show. Will you mount an exhibit which will show the various uses of fans, their evolution, their changes, their artistic differences? Will you indicate, through them, that they were used as cooling equipment, as flirtatious devices, as accessories to women's fashion? Will the display be of fans? Or will you use only one or two of them in a display of women's clothing generally, to indicate their function as part of a larger picture. How will you use the fans to interpret the past?

Throughout the country there are so-called museums which are merely gathering-places of things, objects jammed together in cases and cupboards with no reason whatsoever, put wherever there was an inch of space. How much more effective they would be if the material were displayed, not crammed!

Before you begin to organize your displays, consider first what their purpose is. What will they show? Then do whatever background research you need so that you will know about what each item was, its purpose, its date of common usage, all that you need to know about them. Finally, then, it is time to put the exhibit together. If yours is a group depending on volunteers, try to find someone who prepares displays for a local store, or is otherwise familiar with merchandising techniques, to help you with your exhibits.

Labeling should be done systematically and in a pleasing manner. No matter how small, how impoverished your museum, take the time and energy, and money, to have your exhibits properly labeled so that viewers can understand what they are looking at.

Do the proper research to know what each item in the display is, what period it represents, what it is made of, what makes it

This museum exhibit of harness equipment shows the viewer what an early-day harness shop looked like. The enlarged photograph in the center shows the original shop, and the legends describe what the various items on display are. This display interprets history.

particularly valuable historically—and finally, where it came from or who gave it to you. Encyclopedias from the local library are a good starting point for information; from there, you can use technical magazines and other sources. Be sure you are accurate in your labels.

Use cards of standard material and color, and lettering that is also standard for your labels. Either have them hand-lettered by a professional, or run off on a regular lettering machine. Perhaps you can make arrangements with a local store to use its lettering equipment in off-hours, until you can afford to buy one yourself.

The labels themselves should be terse, succinct, so that viewers will read them; few people will stop to read a legend of a hundred words. The display of fans, for instance, could have one general label, saying "Victorian ladies found many uses for fans," and then separate labels could tell what they were: ". . . for cooling her brow," or ". . . for flirting," or ". . . for hiding her blushes." In the corner of each, in smaller lettering, you could indicate the approximate date of each one, and the name of the donor.

Whenever possible, each item should carry its own label. Avoid the system of small numbers that must be keyed to a list or catalog; few of your viewers will take the time to study the reference, and your otherwise carefully planned display will lose its effectiveness as an interpretive instrument.

The displays of one fine small local museum in mid-America lose their impact simply because the labeling is poorly done. Instead of eye-catching labels telling what each item is, the ladies in charge have pinned little pieces of paper to each item, with hand-written notations as to who gave them the old dresses, old bonnets, old silver serving pieces. There is no description at all, and the cheap, amateur little scraps of paper make the whole roomful of displays look temporary and uninviting. Another otherwise fine local museum has many labels misspelled, and the viewer tends to doubt the accuracy of them altogether.

There are many more matters to consider about a museum, once you establish it and get it functioning. You should take proper measures for security, including some sort of burglar detection equipment. When you begin to install your exhibits, be sure that they are screwed into place—screws are better than nails—and that all parts of the museum are visible to the attendants on duty. If you have volunteer helpers, make sure they have a sense of dedication so that they are on duty according to schedule.

The building will have to follow the rules of local and state fire laws and of the Occupational Safety and Health Act (OSHA) regulations.

For a more effective museum in general, you will need detailed knowledge about specialized lighting in exhibits, for instance, and for the preservation of delicate items, the restoring of others.

Books and technical leaflets from the American Association for State and Local History, curatorial advice through their consultative service, and all other sorts of help are available.

The American Association of Museums, the Smithsonian, the National Archives, and the American Association for State and Local History sponsor workshops and seminars on various specialized subjects to help personnel in local museums; they are a good means of learning new techniques, new procedures, and of assessing your own accomplishments against those of institutions similar to your own.

A museum is not a static thing; it must grow and develop to be of service to the community.

OTHER HELP AVAILABLE

Published by American Association for State and Local History:
Introduction to Museum Work, by G. Ellis Burcaw.
The Management of Small History Museums, by Carl E. Guthe.
The Care of Historical Collections, by Per G. Guldbeck.
Available from AASLH:
Help! for the Small Museum, by Arminta Neal.
A Primer on Museum Security, by Keck et al.
A Bibliography on Historical Organization Practices: Historic Preservation. by Frederick L. Rath, Jr., and Merrilyn R. O'Connell.
AASLH Technical Leaflet 4, *Methods, Materials, Bibliography*.
AASLH Technical Leaflet 56, *Case Arrangement and Design*.

AASLH Technical Leaflet 52, *Gallery and Case Design*.
AASLH Technical Leaflet 12, *Case and Prop Design*.
AASLH Technical Leaflet 20, *Figures for Miniature Dioramas*.
AASLH Technical Leaflet 49, *Use of Plexiglas*.
AASLH Technical Leaflet 33, *Displaying Costumes*.
AASLH Technical Leaflet 54, *Sponsorship for Exhibits*.
AASLH Technical Leaflet 22, *Hand-Lettering*.
AASLH Technical Leaflet 23, *Three-Dimensional Letters*.
AASLH Technical Leaflet 60, *Content of Exhibit Labels*.
AASLH Technical Leaflet 64, *Constructing Life-Size Figures*.
AASLH Technical Leaflet 68, *A Silk Screening Facility*.
AASLH Technical Leaflet 69, *Preparing Exhibit Mock-ups*.
AASLH Technical Leaflet 46, *Organizing a Museum Store*.
AASLH Technical Leaflet 71, *Care of Textiles and Costumes: Adaptive Techniques for Basic Maintenance*.
AASLH Technical Leaflet 73, *Exhibit Planning: Ordering Your Artifacts Interpretively*.
AASLH Technical Leaflet 75, *The Exhibit of Documents: Preparation, Matting and Display Techniques*.
AASLH Technical Leaflet 78, *Planning a Local Museum: An Approach for Historical Societies*.

How to Use Volunteers

All historical societies, large or small, depend in large degree on the services of willing, dedicated volunteers to help with their programs. Small historical societies are absolutely dependent upon them.

Your own officers, directors and members will of course administer the bulk of your activities. But there are many other persons in the community who will be available and willing to help you, if you know how to find them and utilize their services.

Even before you issue a call for volunteers, have specified assignments, specific duties, for them to fill. Make lists of work you need to have done—job descriptions. Then make lists of specifications of workers for those specific jobs—job requirements and preparation. Some work is suitable for young people with active, vigorous bodies and not much historical expertise; some for eager young history students; other work is more appropriate for retirees, with time, patience, and detailed knowledge of the community in the past.

Sources of volunteers are many. Boy Scout and Girl Scout groups have merit badge programs for historical service; other youth groups are also available. Service clubs, such as Rotary, Kiwanis, Optimists and others, can supply manpower, as can women's clubs of various kinds. Retirement programs, either organized into groups such as Retired Senior Volunteer Program

(R.S.V.P.), Committees on Aging, or members of senior citizens' communities are also good sources for volunteers. In addition, persons who are not members of any organized group are often interested in history and have the time and inclination to help with historical societies.

Before you begin your own program using volunteer services, you may wish to ask a few persons to help you on an experimental basis, to see how you will utilize their services. Most organizations who rely on volunteer helpers have discovered that their programs work better if every person has a schedule and is on duty at a given time each week; otherwise, they say, nobody shows up on Monday and too many people on Thursday. On the other hand, other organizations report that if volunteers feel that they are tied down to a specific schedule, they won't commit themselves at all; they would rather work when it's convenient for them. You will have to experiment with your own particular situation before you find exactly the solution for your group.

Having found a working arrangement, then you may want to organize your volunteers into a group with a name—Friends of the Historical Society, or some-such—and find a bookkeeper who keeps track of hours. Even in volunteer service, the competitive spirit prevails, and some persons will work far more than they otherwise would to make sure their names are at the top of the list of volunteer hours! Once a year, you will probably have some sort of ceremony to confer pins or some other sort of recognition on the volunteers who have contributed a given number of hours of service, or more, to the historical society the past 12 months. This is your way of saying thank you for their help, and in the process the ceremony draws attention to your work and fosters goodwill in the community.

What are specific jobs for volunteers? There are as many as there are jobs at all to do. You will need many volunteer typists to help transcribe tape recordings of interviews, to type index cards for your library, to type forms and handle other office details. You will need volunteers to serve as guides, if you have a museum, or as librarians if you have a library. You can use volunteers to help identify pictures, to index newspaper clippings and documents, to do research on historical sites, to do whatever needs to be done.

Volunteers should never be considered people to do merely busy work and menial tasks; they should be assigned real responsibilities, utilizing their abilities to the utmost.

The best programs challenge volunteers with responsibility, and therefore those programs require much staff work to make them successful. When your volunteers arrive on duty, have specific jobs assigned to them, with someone in charge to whom they may address questions. They will need to know exactly how to do their work, and will in many cases need to know why it is to be done; someone needs to be present to supervise their work to make the most effective use of their time and talents. Let them

Volunteer docents listen to a lecture on the Victorian glassware and decorative items in the museum collection. They will be able to explain and interpret the artifacts more accurately with their increased knowledge.

develop within their own abilities; they will be the backbone of your organization.

If you will use many volunteers in one specific field—as museum guides, for instance—it would be worthwhile to have detailed training courses for them, to tell them, at one time, what their duties and responsibilities are.

If yours is a historical society with a professional staff, and if there is a college or university in your area, it may be possible for you to work out an intern program with the college, in which competent history majors can work with your professional staff, as unpaid assistants, in return for college credit. The college is getting, in reality, a professional instructor for a few students, the historical society is getting trainable services, and the students are getting on-the-job training in professional historianship, with college credit to boot. The internship program is carefully supervised by the college history department, to insure professionalism on all sides, and in situations where the program has been initiated, it has been of great mutual benefit to all persons involved. Work-study programs of utilizing student help are relatively inexpensive, if your society can come up with the matching funds.

From your ranks of volunteers will come new members for your board of directors, new members for your society, and new enthusiasm for your entire undertaking in the community. Your volunteer program supplies help you need in carrying out your projects, and it also helps publicize your work generally. You might also investigate the possibility of volunteers from local companies to help with construction work, wiring and plumbing. With shorter working hours, longer vacation periods, and earlier retirement years, many people in any given community are looking for challenging, stimulating ways to invest leisure time. They are looking for your historical society.

OTHER HELP AVAILABLE

AASLH Technical Leaflet 65, *Training Docents*.
Interpretation of Historic Sites, by William T. Alderson and Shirley P. Low, American Association for State and Local History.

Publishing

The spoken word dissipates into the air; the written word remains.

Whether your publishing is merely typing and preserving well written accurately documented manuscripts of activities of the past, or a full-scale publishing program, you should consider that the writing of history is an important part of your activity.

The printed word must be accurate

Anything that is published—put into print—will assume great importance historically. "It's in print, so it must be right" is a common assumption. Be sure that everything you write is accurate: names, dates, relationships, names of activities, everything. Document it, if not in the printed version, at least in something that is in your files so that you can check back, in years to come, to the source material. Footnote it somehow.

Much of the support for many local historical societies comes from persons who have grown up in the community and moved away, but have a nostalgic feeling for their home towns. They especially appreciate whatever historical material is published, for it is really all that they get for their membership dues.

On the other hand, many newcomers in the community want to know something of the background of the town where they live. They also are interested in published material.

Your historical writing and publishing may be on a regular basis—quarterly magazines, annuals, monthlies—or may be a once-in-a-lifetime detailed book, or both. Whatever it is, be sure it is accurate. If your historical society does not have funds to do publishing itself, perhaps it could make arrangements with the local newspaper to print stories of a historical nature at regular intervals. You could supply suggestions for topics and do the basic research, if necessary; if the stories come from your own organization, you will have more assurance that they are accurate than if a staff reporter, particularly one unfamiliar with local history, writes them. Sometimes, however, you will discover that reporters long resident in the community may be far more knowledgeable about local history than some of your own members. If you take the time to establish good rapport with your local newspaper, you will discover that the staff will be happy to cooperate with the historical society.

Historical writing

Periodicals

If you have the manpower available and the financing possible for a publication which appears on a regular schedule, you will discover that your historical society has something to offer its members, both locally and at a distance, which will stimulate interest in your entire program.

The stories in your publication can be more detailed than those you would publish in an overall history, they can be on less serious subjects but ones which are nevertheless important. This undertaking—since it is a continuous project—can be more flexible than the ordinary feature.

But the research and writing should be carefully done. Each story should be well documented and accurate, although it should be written in an easy-to-read style, not a dry pedantic one. History can be fun, and you can make it so in your periodical.

The subject matter should be thought-provoking, and specific. Rather than a story on "How Our Forefathers Lived," have stories on "Christmas in the 1880s," or "When Crystal Set Radios Were in Vogue," or "When Polio Struck Smith County." Try to vary the topics so that you will appeal to a wide public and have them represent different periods of history. Stories which your members can relate to, of matters they remember from their own past or have heard about from their parents, attract much interest. For one issue, for instance, you could have a story about dinner parties in your community during the Victorian era, including menus and descriptions of tablesettings, and for another one, a story about how the town fared during the flu epidemic after World War I. Both are historical but represent two entirely different subjects and periods of time. Various depressions, particularly the one of the 1930s, are good subject matter since they are now historical and many of your readers can remember specific details from their own lives. The subject matter is unlimited.

For source material, use newspapers, books, scrapbooks, interviews, legal records, deathbooks in the City Hall (particularly good for the flu epidemic story), and anything else you can find. One historical society puts a letter to the editor in the local newspaper from time to time telling what subject it is working on now, with an appeal to the public for information or pictures; this use of publicity brings forth specific historical material and stimulates great interest in the forthcoming issues of its periodical.

Historical societies which have museum programs can often correlate the stories in the periodicals with existing exhibits or those in preparation, to serve as a catalog as well as a history-telling medium.

There is no one particular format for a publication that is better than any other. Some local historical societies, such as in San Diego, publish magazine-sized quarterlies, occasionally using colored illustrations; others, such as in Greenbrier, West Virginia, publish once a year. The Adams County, Nebraska, society publishes a 6-page monthly. Some have mimeographed booklets. The size, format and frequency of publication vary with the financial ability of the organization, the purpose of the publication, and the ability of the staff.

One small local historical society uses 6-page monthly publications for its publishing program, each issue having well-researched, brightly-written stories. Topics through the years have ranged from stories of Indian raids and early settlers, a series on Prohibition starting with temperance societies and going up through the bootlegging era, ethnic groups, gypsies, beauty parlors, and many others; they encompass a wide span of years historically and a great variety of subjects. One page each month is set aside for news of the society, the single publication serving as both a historical magazine and as a newsletter. Every 3 years the stories from the preceding 36 issues are reprinted in paperback.

The editor should be well trained, knowledgeable in English grammar and composition as well as in history; if you must rely on a volunteer for editing service, consider a newspaper reporter, or an English or history teacher, or someone else in the community who writes well and is interested in historical details. As your publication gains momentum, contributors will be eager to submit their work; all of the material should be factual, well reasoned and written in a simple, readable, easy style. The editor should reserve the right to make any necessary corrections in the manuscript for clarity, and to reject manuscripts which do not meet the standards of the publication. In lieu of payment, your contributors will have by-lines on their stories.

When it is time to begin technical work on the publication itself, work closely with your printer. If he has someone on his staff who is a professional designer, ask for suggestions about the most efficient printing procedures; he will know the page sizes which will be the most practicable for the press and for paper trimming, the type size that will be the most readable, and other details which will help you have a well designed, professional-looking publication for the least amount of money. You should not choose your printer solely on the basis of the cheapest bid; there are other considerations which may make that choice of printer penny-wise and dollar-foolish.

Modern offset printing techniques make the use of pictures economically feasible, and good pictorial content adds much to a story. Be sure every picture is identified so that your readers will know what it is about, and give credit for the source.

If your publication is newspaper style which may not be durable enough for posterity, you may wish to consider reprints every few years in book form, either paperback or hardback. If you decide this before you publish your first issue, taking into consideration book size as well as regular publication size, the printer can save the negatives for future use. One historical society which publishes a monthly paper issues a book of reprints every three years and enjoys a modest income from the sale of them; many of those who buy the books are persons who enjoyed the original stories and are pleased to have them in bound form.

If your publication is a more or less standard state historical quarterly size, you may wish to consider offering hardbound copies every 3 or 4 years, collecting together enough to make a significant volume.

If you have a continuous publishing program, you will want to consider an index to be published at regular intervals, every year, every 5 years, or whatever seems to be a workable period. See the section below for details on indexing procedures.

Detailed historical books

A comprehensive history of your community is a large project which requires tremendous organization, considerable financing, and huge quantities of hard work. Before you consider plunging into such an endeavor, be sure you realize all of the hard work and attention to detail that preparing such a volume entails.

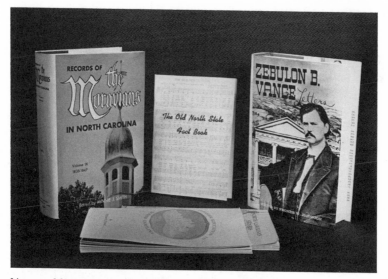

Your publication may be a big one with a hard-back cover and much detail, or it may be a more modest paperback. No matter the size, the book should be carefully organized and every detail in it should be accurate. Whatever is in print will be looked to as the definitive source of history for years to come.

Start with its organization. Will you organize it topically, with one chapter dealing with governmental development, another on education, another on business and industry, another on churches? Will it be organized chronologically, by stages of development in everything? Will you show a cause-and-effect relationship, or merely recount what happened with no attempt at interpretation?

Whatever organizational framework you choose, arrange your book so that it has unity and sequence. Many local histories in the past have been hodgepodge compilations of individual stories, one having no relationship to the next; those volumes do have historical value, to be sure, but could have much more if they had been organized in an orderly fashion.

You will need a general editor or writer who will have final authority, and many volunteers to help with research, documenting everything they submit. Assign one group to churches, for instance, and another group to schools, and a third one to businesses, allowing each one enough time to collect material but with a definite deadline so that they will not dawdle. Tell them that their job is to make an exhaustive search for all possible material; it is far better to have too much information than not enough. All of the source material you will eventually put into your permanent files.

Go to original sources whenever possible, rather than relying on previously written books; you do not want to perpetuate old mistakes, if those authors have made errors in dates or spellings or of fact. One local history author discovered that a book written in 1916, previously assumed to be the historical authority of the area, contained large quantities of material from a volume published in 1890, which in turn copied from a book of 1882; in checking courthouse records, city hall records, and other original sources, she discovered that the author of the 1882 book had miscopied legal records in some cases, exaggerated stories in others, and had made the monumental mistakes which had been carried on for years.

If you have a topical organization for the book, with separate chapters on various institutions, work out form letters which you can mimeograph and send out to the various establishments asking for specific information: name, date of organization, founding members, location of original and subsequent buildings, original purpose and any changes therefrom, and all of the other information you think you will need. Ask also for copies of any booklets, pamphlets, and other material they may have in their files. Set a deadline for the return of those forms. But do not take that information as the sum total of what you wish; from there, ask for annual reports, financial statements, minute books, PTA books, ladies-aid records, elders or trustees books, school annuals, and any other records which are available.

While the individual researchers are gathering together all of the specific detailed information, the person who is to be the writer, who is in charge of the volume overall, should be reading the local newspapers, one issue after another in sequence. Even if your history is not arranged in chronological manner, it is well to have an idea of the internal sequence of events. One newspaper by itself doesn't mean much, but when you study the newspapers sequentially for a 10-year span, or even 5 years, you can discover changes in attitudes, in patterns of living, and other subtle developments that do not show up in any other form. You will also make notations of outside influences that affected the town: World War I, for instance, stock market debacles, the advent of television—any happenings outside the community which had a direct bearing on the area, although they did not originate there. You will make only passing references to those, but they are a frame of reference to explain to readers why certain occurrences took place.

Your volunteers will also collect pictures, whether they are the same people who are doing basic research or a separate crew of workers. Those persons will be sure to have the pictures identified carefully at the time they pick them up—writing carefully and lightly on the back in an area where the impressions will not interfere with the picture—and indicating whether they are to be returned, and if so, to whom and where. Make sure the donors understand that it may be several months, or even a year, before the photographs are returned, and when you do return them, have the persons who borrowed them assigned the job of taking them back. (Ideally, of course, you would have copies made of those pictures for your own files; practically, however, it often turns out that you simply don't have enough money for that purpose. Indicate in your captions the source of the pictures—"Photo courtesy W. A. Zilch"—so that if you need to borrow it again, you know where it came from; the acknowledgment will also please the donor and will give him a feeling of having shared in preparing the volume.) Borrowed pictures are a trust, and you should honor it diligently.

Pulling all of the information together and writing it is really a one-man job. If some of your researchers have the ability and the desire to write the material they have gathered, let them; they are familiar with it and can probably do a better job of interpreting it than anyone else could. But reserve the right to edit it so that it is in the same general style as that of the rest of the book. The actual writing should be done in a straight-forward, factual style, so unobtrusive that the reader is not aware of it.

Sources

You will use all of the information you have already collected in your library in preparing your publication. You will discover where the gaps are—in fact, you will probably be horrified to find out how little you have, really,—and you will go out to collect more material. Depending on topics, you will use newspapers, legal records, minute books, school and church records, interviews, and all other sources available for research.

If you are writing a really comprehensive account of your community, there will be material in other locations which will be of use to you. The state historical society will have material, possibly including pictures, and will be able to suggest other sources.

Various state agencies—health, education, industry or Chamber of Commerce, meteorology or climatology, and others—may have statistical data and other information they can supply about your community, historically and to the present. If your state has a State Archivist, consult him about what records are available through his office; the state historical society can tell you whether the state has one and where he is located.

Federal agencies are a source of material about your community, through the national archives and Records Service in Washington, D.C., or the eleven regional branches whose addresses are given in Appendix D. These records include U.S. Census records from 1790 on, including decennial censuses and many others, maps records of federal projects (including dams, war-time projects, WPA-type activities and many others), and a wealth of other material. A booklet, Select List of Publications of the National Archives and Records Service, Washington, D.C., 20408, will tell you about some of the material which is available. Some of the material is available on microfilm, which you can obtain on interlibrary loan from the regional office. (If you have difficulty getting a response from any federal agency, it sometimes works to reroute your request through your congressman or senator; overworked, understaffed agencies reply to letters which are coded as coming from a VIP.)

Federal Census data gives decennial population figures, places of origin, ages and educational attainments of the population at a given time, and all manner of other information; specific censuses, such as in agricultural or industrial areas, tell of farm holdings, crops, livestock, minerals, kinds and sizes of industries and businesses, and a wide variety of other information. It does take time to find out what material is available, and how to get it, but official sources can provide a wealth of primary source material.

Business records are good sources of local history. If you are doing research on various businesses and industries in your community, it is easier if you have someone familiar with business procedures do at least the basic research, if not the actual writing; that individual can interpret the annual reports, bookkeeping records and other business data more easily than someone who is not familiar with such procedures. If there are inventions that have contributed to the changing fortunes of the businesses, be sure to describe them and why they were important; if outside influences affected the growth of the business, tell about them. (Does that company still manufacture buggy whips, or did it change to radio and television antennas?)

Your volunteers will also go over local newspapers to make notations of stories about the specific topics they are researching; they will pay attention to legal advertisements as well as news stories and display advertisements. If your state historical society has microfilmed copies of local newspapers, inquire about possibilities of buying copies of the films for your own use; you will then need an inexpensive microfilm reader. If you can rent or lease a microfilm reader-printer, you will find it saves hours of research time by making it possible to have exact copies of newspaper material.

Other sources of information abound. You are limited only by time and the energy of your researchers. For accounts of local musical and theatrical presentations, of commencement activities, of many community undertakings, scrapbooks are great sources of information, particularly if the compilers dated the entries when they pasted in the programs. Even ticket stubs can provide information; one local historical society writing about a Ku Klux Klan chapter had no idea of where the general meetings were held, for newspaper accounts were sparse and few other records were available, but a ticket stub in an old scrapbook provided that information!   How do you compile the material? Some researchers insist on using cards, in the classic termpaper style, with each card indicating a single subject, a single item, with the source clearly indicated. Others insist just as vehemently on using whatever kinds of paper they have at hand, with whatever kind of note-taking procedure. Follow the system that works best for you and your workers; the important thing is that you do gather the information and know exactly where each bit of it came from originally.

Footnotes

What do you do about footnotes? You want your book to appeal to the public in the community, and ordinary people are often turned off at the sight of little numbers and little type at the bottom of each page; it looks like a textbook! But you also want your book to be a valid historic reference book, with each of the sources adequately marked. How do you reconcile these differing needs?

As you are writing the text, you can subtly insert some source information by saying, for instance, "According to the Imperial

Gazette-Journal of July 26, 1896. . . ." But that is not enough. At the end of the chapter, or at the end of the book, have a separate section for notes; instead of having the footnote figures in the text, indicate the page number, line, and item, if necessary, to which you refer: "page 56, line 4, data from Table VII, page 363, Seventh Census Reports on Population, United States Department of Commerce, 1870." Any other material you would ordinarily put in footnotes you will include here, too; serious students will bless you, and the nonstudent readers will never notice the section at all.

You will, of course, acknowledge lavishly the work of all of your volunteer researchers, through an acknowledgment of all of them by name at the beginning of the book, and also in your section of footnotes, indicating that Mary Zilch did the research for this page or chapter.

Whatever you publish must be accurate, for your book will be the source of local history for generations to come. If you have two or three versions of one event, for instance, you will have to assess which is the most likely one—or in some cases, make references to all of them! You must decide for yourself how to handle controversial subjects, remembering that the sin of omission is as wicked as the sin of commission. Your crew will need tact, finesse, brass—and endurance!

Choosing a printer

Your choice of printer for the local history book is important, for the job is a big one and the book you produce will be the definitive history of your community for a long period of time. In most cases, it's 50 or even 100 years between publication of local history volumes; you will want to have a book that will be worthy graphically of your efforts. Do not scrimp in the printing of your book.

If there is no printer available locally to handle the job—and book printing is a special art—make inquiries from the state historical society and other organizations which have had recent publishing experience. Ask them who they have used for printing, for their recommendations; it is also important to find out who they do not recommend! Ask about the quality of work each of the printers turns out, their reliability, and their adherence to deadlines. One local historical society discovered midway through the production of their book that the printer, a student-operated shop which was part of a technical college, was going out of business; the society had to scurry around to find someone else to finish the job, causing a delay of almost a year, and resulting in two different kinds of typefaces and a book whose total appearance was not commensurate with the editorial quality of the volume. Other groups have experienced unconscionable delays in printing.

Talk to many printers even before you ask for bids from them. See what kind of technical help they will be able to give. Do they have book designers on the staff? Will they make arrangements for binding, or will you need to do that? Will they work willingly with you, take a pride in the job—or will they merely consider this just another job to crank out between others? Try to determine before you ask for bids which printers are the ones you think you would be most happy working with. Look at samples of other books they have printed, and even talk to persons responsible for those books to see if they have been satisfied with the service they have had.

When you get to the point of asking for bids or estimates from printers, make sure that all the estimates are based on the same terms and qualifications: cost of typesetting, page makeup, printing; the number of copies; the same page-size, type size, paper quality, pictorial content—and the screen or quality of pictures (the higher the number of lines in the screen, the finer the quality of pictures, and the higher the cost); and a clear determination of responsibilities. Does the printer read proof, or do you; does he make the dummy layout, or do you? Does he arrange for binding—and will it be soft-cover or hardbound. If it is soft-cover, what sort of gluing or stitching, and it it is hardbound, will it have headbands (extra stitching glued in for durability) and what will be the weight of the boards, the quality of buckram?

If you are obligated by law to accept the lowest bid, be especially sure that the estimate sheets cover every possible con-

tingency; many low-bid jobs are low simply because the esti-
mator is figuring the cheapest quality and not including professional services the customer has every right to expect from a
printer.

When you draw up a contract with the printer, be sure all of
these items are written in, so that you will not end up with
inferior paper quality or some other substitution that will dis-
may you. Deadlines should be clearly stated, both for the delivery of copy from you and for the delivery of the printed, finished
volume. Do not rush through the task of selecting and negotiat-
ing with your printer. The job that he does will stay on the
bookshelf for a long time; you will want to be sure that his work
will be something you can be proud of.

On your part, make sure the manuscript is complete in all
details before you turn it in, and that it is marked according to
the printer's instructions so that there are no ambiguities in
direction. Changes cost money.

Indexing

After the manuscript is at the printer's shop, you must begin
one of the most important parts of the book—the index. For a
historical volume, especially, is no better than its index, for that
is the reference your readers and scholars need to locate the
information they want.

The printer sets the manuscript into type, then makes proofs
which are read and corrected, and finally puts the type into page
form. The pages are arranged in segments called *signatures*,
which are 8, 16 or 32 pages in size, depending on press and page
sizes, with each page numbered as it will be in the book. Ask the
printer to make two proofs of each signature, one for you to make
a last-minute check on—to be sure that pictures are turned right
side around, that the proper pictures are on each page, and that
everything is exactly as you want it in the finished book. Check it
over carefully, marking any necessary corrections, initial it, and
return it to the printer. The second copy you will use to compile
your index.

Possibly the easiest way to read the book for indexing purposes is to use a ruler so that you can read the page line by line, making notations on a ruled sheet of paper about the information in each line of the book.

"Jones, Harry A., city councilman, stand on Sunday movies, 1913, p. 374," might be one entry.

"Sunday movies, stand of Harry A. Jones, 1913, p. 374" might be another entry for the same line of text.

"Movies, Sunday, stand of Harry A. Jones, councilman, 1913, p. 374," could be another entry.

"Recreation: see Movies," could be still a fourth index entry for that one line of text in the book.

If you have time for more than one person to index each signature, you will have a double check on entries for the index; even when indexes are prepared by professional index compilers they often are not detailed enough! Librarians, teachers who have had library science courses in cataloguing, and persons who have done considerable research and know from experience what general topics they look for, all are likely candidates for volunteer help in preparing your index.

After the listings have been made on lined paper, have volunteer typists prepare cards, one entry to a card, and file the cards alphabetically.

Finally, weeks later, after all the signatures of the book have been combed for index entries, and all of the cards have been alphabetized, it is time to compile the index as it should be for the printer. One historical society had an Index-Typing Day, gathering twenty typists in a large office room, each typist taking a separate letter of the alphabet. Mrs. Roberts typed the A's, Mrs. Nelson the B 's, Mrs. Berger the C's; Mr. Hansen took the Q's, and X-Y-Z's! The whole typing procedure took 4 hours of time with twenty persons working together, sharing the experience and making their contribution to the work.

Index the book in as much detail as possible; try to project yourself into the place of a researcher 50 years from now who is trying to find specific details in your volume. History students will want to know where people's names are, where specific issues are mentioned, where general topics are discussed. You will make general entries; for instance, under "Schools," you may want to make "also see" entries, such as "see athletics," or "see music," or "see population," for entries in those classifications that have relevance to the general subject of schools. The more detail you have in your index, the more useful the index is; rather than merely saying "Irrigation, p. 283," it is better to say "Irrigation, public meeting about legal problems, 1967, p. 283."

Indexing is sometimes tedious, but it is essential to any volume on local history. Allow plenty of time for it.

Financing

How do you finance a publishing program?

In the case of regular periodicals, publishing costs can come from your regular budget, with your membership fees covering the subscription price. You will need to apply at the post office for a Postal Permit for a Nonprofit Organization, Bulk Rate for Mailing, or a Second Class Mailing Permit which also has a special nonprofit category.

For a detailed historical volume, you certainly will need financing beyond your own treasury. This can come from grants from the city or county government, revenue-sharing funds (if there are any), Chamber of Commerce help or local business support—banks, local businesses and industries, alumni funds, or prepublication sales. The chapter on finances may suggest other sources.

How do you figure the selling price of a book so that you can take orders before publication? First of all, you need to know how many copies of the book to have printed, and then figure the cost per book, based on the total printing bill, advertising costs and whatever else you will spend in production and promotion. Price each book at least three times its actual cost, so that you do not have to sell every copy to have sufficient money to pay the printer.

The determination of how many copies to have printed is partly scientific study but largely guesswork; as a rule of thumb, you should figure on having the books available for sale over a 20-year period. Local county histories are not best sellers; they have their greatest burst of sales in the first year or two after they are published. But because of their very nature, they do have continuous sales—smaller ones, to be sure—over a long period of time as genealogists, grandchildren of old-timers, history buffs, and others hear about them. Some overly conservative editors figure too short, and have to order reprints of their books in a year or two, a procedure more costly than if they had ordered a sufficient number when the books were on the press; other overly enthusiastic souls order an unrealistically high number, more than they could sell in a century. Consider how many people now live in the community, what percentages of families—not individuals—would be interested in buying the book, and how many you will be able to sell to old-timers now living elsewhere; possibly half your sales, or more, will come from outside the immediate area, from persons nostalgic about the Old Home Town.

One local historical society made a concentrated sales effort before the book went to the printer, and from prepublication sales made enough money to pay almost the entire costs. That group was unusual, however; most must rely on outside help to underwrite the publishing costs. In a few unfortunate situations, the editor or writer has ended up signing a note himself at the bank to cover printing costs, in the hopes of getting the money back from sales. This procedure is not recommended.

Only as a last resort should you consider selling and printing advertisements from local concerns; with advertisements, the volume is not so much of a history book as it is an extension of a high school annual. If it seems, however, that that means is the only way to raise enough money to print a local history, be sure to have an Internal Revenue Service ruling about that revenue before you begin.

Merchandising

How do you merchandise your publications?

For your periodicals, get alumni lists from the local schools and send well-written letters to out-of-town graduates, playing on nostalgia, telling them about your publication, even possibly enclosing a sample copy. Be sure the application blank lists the membership price. Get lists of newcomers from the Chamber of

Commerce, real-estate agents, Welcome Wagon, or utility meter-deposit lists, and send letters and possibly sample copies to newcomers.

See that every organization in town has a copy which is distributed at a meeting so that members can see it, and will know how to join the society. Have a copy at the local library, for people to see; if it's on the reference shelf, not to be checked out, you will get more subscription orders than if the patron can take it home and read it free!

Have copies available in all school libraries.

Have copies of your periodical and subscription forms wherever people are—grocery stores, filling stations, department stores, bulletin boards—so that people can see them, know the subscription figure, and can subscribe easily.

Have your publications available at your own sales desk, of course, and at all tourist stops in the area—motel bookstands, highway cafes, filling stations. Tourists will often buy books or pamphlets faster than townspeople will, simply to know about the area they are in now; the home-towners already know.

For your detailed history book, you will need even more specific merchandising techniques.

Have leaflets printed describing your book—how big it is, what it covers, how many pictures it has—and distributed in the same places mentioned for periodicals. Tell where it can be bought, and for how much. People will fill in coupons faster than they will write a note; have coupons available.

Send review copies to book editors of the newspaper in your area; send a review copy to the state historical society suggesting they review it in their publication. If you think the book is of unusual significance historically, send review copies to other historical organizations which publish.

If you have enough critical reviews to be encouraging, prepare a printed brochure—it will cost money!—and mail copies to schools, libraries and colleges in the area; also send those flyers to persons on your alumni lists.

Try to gear your publication date for Christmas, or for a time when the community is having some sort of anniversary celebration which will draw attention to the past. Have your book new and fresh and sparkling at a time when people will want to buy it.

Try to arrange a window display in your local book store or department store, and an autographing party at a specific time in that store.

Talk to history and social studies teachers in the schools, to see if there is some way to coordinate efforts; it may be possible from time to time for them to make assignments from the book. You will, of course, have given copies of the volumes to all of the school libraries in the area, as a goodwill gesture.

Use all the facilities at your command to publicize it; arrange interviews for the author or committee with newspapers, Sunday magazines, radio and television programs. You have spent much effort and money to produce the book; don't be shy about promoting it.

One of the most exciting things on earth is your first look at your newly-printed, newly-bound book!

Newsletters

Most historical societies will need to publish newsletters from time to time to advise their members about activities and programs.

These newsletters are not about history; they are about the historical society. They should be thought of as "what we're up to now" publications, and should be carefully prepared, both in content and form. They project your society to your public; a sloppy newsletter indicates a careless, less than first rate historical society.

Newsletters may be mimeographed or printed, and should be attractive in appearance and interesting in content. They include scheduled events, lists of committee members, assignments for volunteers, plans being formulated, duns for membership dues, and other information necessary for the efficient operation of the society.

They also give follow-up stories about completed programs: how much money was raised by the carnival, how many persons attended a program, how many persons went on a tour, how many members have now joined. They can include requests for specific items for a particular museum display, for information about a definite subject, for suggestions about specific projects in the future.

Newsletters are the means by which the society and its members keep in touch. The larger the society membership, the greater the need for this means of communication. If yours is a small local historical society with limited means, which also has a regular historical periodical, you can consider using one publication for both purposes, using the same page in every issue for historical society information. The same postal permit requirements apply to newsletters as to other historical periodicals.

Other publishing

From time to time, your historical society will be involved with other publishing, whether it is brochures about the museum, catalogs of your collections, maps (see chapter 5), leaflets, or any of a dozen or so other publishing projects.

By now you will have established a good rapport with a printer, one who has the facilities and the desire to help you plan your printing. You have confidence in him and you will keep in close touch with him, paying attention to details.

You have your logo, or identifying mark which people associate with your historical society, and you use it in varying sizes in all of your publishing endeavors, so that readers automatically associate your society with the publication.

You realize that anything which is printed under your name will project the image of your group to the public. Whatever you publish that is about history is accurate, carefully researched, carefully documented. Whatever you publish at all is well written and grammatical, attractive in appearance, with neatness and aesthetic appeal. You do not take shortcuts nor settle for less than the best, for you want the public to know that your historical society is a quality one.

OTHER HELP AVAILABLE

Researching, Writing, and Publishing Local History, by Thomas E. Felt, American Association for State and Local History.

Newsletter Techniques, an audio-visual training kit, by staff of American Association for State and Local History.

AASLH Technical Leaflet 34, *Publishing*.

AASLH Technical Leaflet 39, *Newsletters*.

AASLH Technical Leaflet 51, *Marking and Correcting Copy*.

AASLH Technical Leaflet 53, *Spotting Mechanical Errors in Proof*.

Appendix A

State Historical Societies

Agencies most likely to answer general questions about historical society activities in the state.

Alabama Department of Archives and History
624 Washington Avenue
Montgomery, Alabama 36104

Alaska Historical Library
Pouch G, State Capitol
Juneau, Alaska 99801

Arizona State Department of Library and Archives
3rd Floor, State Capitol
Phoenix, Arizona 85007

Arkansas Historical Association
History Department
University of Arkansas
Fayetteville, Arkansas 72703

Arkansas History Commission
300 West Markham Street
Little Rock, Arkansas 72201

Historical Society of Southern California
200 East Avenue 43
Los Angeles, California 90031

California Department of Parks and Recreation
Box 2390
Sacramento, California 95811

California Historical Society
2090 Jackson Street
San Francisco, California 94115

Conference of California Historical Societies
University of the Pacific
Stockton, California 95204

State Historical Society of Colorado
200 14th Avenue
Denver, Colorado 80203

Connecticut Historical Society
1 Elizabeth Street
Hartford, Connecticut 06105

Historical Society of Delaware
501 Market Street
Wilmington, Delaware 19801

American Historical Association
400 A Street, S.E.
Washington, D.C. 20003

Florida Division of Archives, History and Records Management
401 E. Gaines Street
Tallahassee, Florida 32301

Florida Historical Society
University of Florida Library
Tampa, Florida 33620

Georgia Department of Archives and History
330 Capitol Avenue
Atlanta, Georgia 30334

Georgia Historical Commission
116 Mitchell Street, S.W.
Atlanta, Georgia 30303

Bernice P. Bishop Museum
1355 Kalihi Street
Honolulu, Hawaii 96818

Idaho State Historical Society
610 North Julia Davis Drive
Boise, Idaho 83706

Illinois State Historical Library
Old State Capitol
Springfield, Illinois 62706

Indiana Historical Bureau
State Library and Historical Building
Indianapolis, Indiana

Iowa State Department of History and Archives
East 12th Street and Grand Ave.
Des Moines, Iowa 50319

Kansas State Historical Society
Memorial Building
120 West 10th Street
Topeka, Kansas 66612

Kentucky Historical Society
Box H
Frankfort, Kentucky 40601

Louisiana Historical Association
Box 44422, Capitol Station
Baton Rouge, Louisiana 70804

Maine Historical Society
485 Congress Street
Portland, Maine 04111

Maryland Historical Society
Baltimore, Maryland 21202

Massachusetts Historical Society
1154 Boylston Street
Boston, Massachusetts 02215

Massachusetts Historical Commission
Office of the Secretary
State House
Boston, Massachusetts 02133

Bay State Historical League
Box 255
North Andover, Massachusetts 01845

Division of Michigan History
208 North Capitol Avenue
Mutual Building
Lansing, Michigan 48933

Minnesota Historical Society
690 Cedar Street
St. Paul, Minnesota 55101

Mississippi Historical Society
Box 571
Jackson, Mississippi 39205

Missouri Historical Society
Jefferson Memorial Building
St. Louis, Missouri 63112

Montana Historical Society
225 North Roberts
Helena, Montana 59601

Nebraska State Historical Society
1500 R Street
Lincoln, Nebraska 68508

Nevada State Historical Society
1650 North Virginia Street
Reno, Nevada 89504

New Hampshire Historical Society
30 Park Street
Concord, New Hampshire 03301

League of Historical Societies of New Jersey
Box 531
Elizabeth, New Jersey 07207

New Jersey Historical Commission
State Library
185 West State Street
Trenton, New Jersey 08625

Museum of New Mexico
Box 2087
113 Lincoln
Santa Fe, New Mexico 87501

New York Office of the State Historian
New York State Museum
Albany, New York 12210

New York State Historical Association
Box 391, Lake Road
Cooperstown, New York 13326

North Carolina State Division of Archives and History
109 East Jones Street
Raleigh, North Carolina 27611

State Historical Society of North Dakota
Liberty Memorial Building
Bismark, North Dakota 58501

Ohio Historical Society
Ohio Historical Center
Columbus, Ohio 43211

Oklahoma Historical Society
Historical Building, Capital Sub-station
Oklahoma City, Oklahoma 73105

Oregon Historical Society
1230 S.W. Park Avenue
Portland, Oregon 97205

Pennsylvania Historical and Museum Commission
Box 1026
Harrisburg, Pennsylvania 17108

Rhode Island Historical Society
52 Power Street
Providence, Rhode Island 02906

South Carolina Department of Archives and History
1430 Senate Street
Columbia, South Carolina 29211

South Dakota State Historical Society
Soldiers' and Sailors' Memorial Building
East Capital Avenue
Pierre, South Dakota 57501

Tennessee Historical Commission
403 7th Avenue North
Nashville, Tennessee 37219

Texas Library and Historical Commission
1201 Brazos, Box 12927
Austin, Texas 78711

Texas State Historical Association
Sid Richarson Hall 2/306
University Station
Austin, Texas 78712

Texas State Historical Survey Committee
108 West 15th Street
Austin, Texas 78711

Utah State Historical Society
603 East South Temple
Salt Lake City, Utah 84102

Vermont Historical Society
Pavilion Building
Montpelier, Vermont 05602

Virginia Historic Landmarks Commission
1116 9th Street
State Office Building
Richmond, Virginia 23219

Virginia Historical Society
428 North Boulevard, Box 7311
Richmond, Virginia 23221

Eastern Washington State Historical Society
West 2316 1st Avenue
Spokane, Washington 99204

Washington State Historical Society
315 North Stadium Way
Tacoma, Washington 98403

West Virginia Department of Archives and History
400 East Wing
State Capitol
Charleston, West Virginia 25305

State Historical Society of Wisconsin
816 State Street
Madison, Wisconsin 53706

Wyoming State Archives and Historical Department
State Office Building
Cheyenne, Wyoming 82001

Canada
Provincial Historical Agencies

Alberta
Historical Society of Alberta
Box 4481, Station C
Calgary, Alberta T2T SN3

Provincial Museum and Archives of Alberta
12845 102nd Avenue
Edmonton, Alberta T5N 0M6

British Columbia
British Columbia Provincial Museum
Heritage Court
601 Belleville Street
Victoria, B.C.

New Brunswick
New Brunswick Museum
277 Douglas Avenue
Saint John, New Brunswick

Nova Scotia
Nova Scotia Historical Society
c/o The Public Archives of Nova Scotia
Coburg Road
Halifax, Nova Scotia

Nova Scotia Museum
1747 Summer Street
Halifax, Nova Scotia

Ontario
National Museums of Canada
Ottawa, Ontario K1A 0M8

Public Archives of Canada
395 Wellington Street
Ottawa, Ontario K1A 0N3

Ontario Historical Society
1466 Bathurst Street
Toronto, Ontario M5R 3J3

Quebec
Institut Canadien de Quebec
37 Rue Sainte-Angele
Quebec, Quebec

Saskatchewan
Saskatchewan Museum of Natural History
Wascana Park
Regina, Saskatchewan

Saskatchewan Archives Board
University of Saskatchewan
Library Building
Regina, Saskatchewan S7N 0W0

Appendix B

State Arts Agencies

Alabama State Council on the Arts and Humanities
322 Alabama Street
Montgomery, Alabama 36104
205/269-7804

Alaska State Council on the Arts
Fifth Floor, MacKay Building
Anchorage, Alaska 99501
907/279-3824

Arizona Commission on the Arts and Humanities
6330 North 7th Street
Phoenix, Arizona 85014
602/271-5884

Arkansas State Council on the Arts and Humanities
400 Train Station Square
Victory at Markham
Little Rock, Arkansas 72201
501/371-1301

California Arts Commission
808 "O" Street
Sacramento, California 95814
916/455-1530

The Colorado Council on the Arts and Humanities
1550 Lincoln Street, Room 205
Denver, Colorado 80203
303/892-2617-8

Connecticut Commission on the Arts
340 Capitol Avenue
Hartford, Connecticut 06106
203/566-4770

Delaware State Arts Council
Room 803, Wilmington Tower
1105 Market Street
Wilmington, Delaware 19801
302/571-3540

District of Columbia Commission on the Arts
Munsey Building, Room 1023
1329 "E" Street, N.W.
Washington, D.C. 20004
202/347-5905

Fine Arts Council of Florida
Department of State
The Capitol Building
Tallahassee, Florida 32304
904/488/2416-7-8-9

Georgia Council for the Arts
706 Peachtree Center South
225 Peachtree Street, N.E.
Atlanta, Georgia 30303
404/656-3990

Hawaii
The State Foundation on Culture and the Arts
250 South Kind Street, Room 310
Honolulu, Hawaii 96813
808/548-4145

Idaho State Commission on the Arts and Humanities
506 N. Fifth Street, Annex #3
Boise, Idaho 83720
208/384-2119

Illinois Arts Council
111 North Wabash Avenue, Room 1610
Chicago, Illinois 60602
312/793-3520

Indiana Arts Commission
155 East Market, Suite 614
Indianapolis, Indiana 46202
317/633-5649

Iowa State Arts Council
State Capitol Building
Des Moines, Iowa 50319
515/281-5297

Kansas Arts Commission
117 West 10th Street, Suite 100
Topeka, Kansas 66612
913/296-3335

Kentucky Arts Commission
Main and High Streets
Frankfort, Kentucky 40601
502/564-3757

Louisiana Council for Music and Performing Arts
International Building
611 Gravier Street
New Orleans, Louisiana 70130
504/525-7241

Maine State Commission on the Arts and Humanities
State House
Augusta, Maine 04330
207/289-2724

Maryland Arts Council
15 West Mulberry Street
Baltimore, Maryland 21201
301/685-7470

Massachusetts Council on the Arts and Humanities
14 Beacon Street
Boston, Massachusetts 02108
617/727-3668

Michigan Council for the Arts
1200 Sixth Avenue
Executive Plaza, Room P160
Detroit, Michigan 48226
313/256-3731

Minnesota State Arts Council
100 East 22nd Street
Minneapolis, Minnesota 55404
612/874-1335

Mississippi Arts Commission
301 North Lamar Street
P.O. Box 1341
Jackson, Mississippi 39205
601/354-7336

Missouri State Council on the Arts
111 South Bemiston, Suite 410
St. Louis, Missouri 63105
314/721-1672

Montana Arts Council
235 East Pine
Missoula, Montana 59801

Nebraska Arts Council
8448 West Center Road
Omaha, Nebraska 68124
402/554-2122

Nevada State Council on the Arts
560 Mill Street
Reno, Nevada 89502
702/784-6231

New Hampshire Commission on the Arts
Phenix Hall
40 North Main Street
Concord, New Hampshire 03301
603/271-2789

New Jersey State Council on the Arts
27 West State Street
Trenton, New Jersey 08625
609/292-6130

New Mexico Arts Commission
Lew Wallace Building, Capitol
Complex
State Capitol
Santa Fe, New Mexico 87501
505/827-2061

New York State Council on the Arts
250 West 57th Street
New York, New York 10019
212/586-2040

North Carolina Arts Council
Department of Cultural
Resources
Raleigh, North Carolina 27611
919/829-7897

**North Dakota Council on the Arts
and Humanities**
North Dakota State University
Department of English
Fargo, North Dakota 58102
701/237-7143

Ohio Arts Council
50 West Broad Street, Suite 2840
Columbus, Ohio 43212
614/466-2613

**Oklahoma Arts and Humanities
Council**
J. M. Thorpe Building
2101 Lincoln Boulevard
Oklahoma City, Oklahoma 73105
405/521-2931-2

Oregon Arts Commission
328 Oregon Building
494 State Street
Salem, Oregon 97301
503/378-3625

**Commonwealth of Pennsylvania
Council on the Arts**
503 North Front Street
Harrisburg, Pennsylvania 17101
717/787-6883

Rhode Island State Council on the Arts
6365 Post Road
East Greenwich, Rhode Island
02818
401/884-6410

South Carolina Arts Commission
Boylston House
829 Richland Street
Columbia, South Carolina 29201
803/758-3443

South Dakota State Fine Arts Council
108 West 11th Street
Sioux Falls, South Dakota 57102
605/339-6647

Tennessee Arts Commission
Capitol Hill Building, Room 222
Nashville, Tennessee 37219
615/741-1701

**Texas Commission on the Arts and
Humanities**
P.O. Box 13406, Capitol Station
202 West 13th Street
Austin, Texas
512/475-6593

Utah State Institute of Fine Arts
609 East South Temple Street
Salt Lake City, Utah 84102
801/328-5895

Vermont Council on the Arts
136 State Street
Montpelier, Vermont 05602
802/828-3291

**Virginia Commission on the Arts and
Humanities**
1215 State Office Building
Richmond, Virginia 23219
804/770-4492

Washington State Arts Commission
1151 Black Lake Boulevard
Olympia, Washington 98504
206/753-3860

West Virginia Arts and Humanities Council
State Office Building No. 6,
Room B-531
1900 Washington Street, East
Charleston, West Virginia 25305
304/348-3711

Wisconsin Arts Board
123 East Washington Avenue
Madison, Wisconsin 53702
608/266-0190

Wyoming Council on the Arts
Cheyenne, Wyomong 82002
307/777-7742

American Samoa Arts Council
Office of the Governor
Pago Pago, American Samoa
96799
Overseas Operator—633-4116

Guam—Insular Arts Council
P.O. Box EK
University of Guam
Agana, Guam 96910
729-2466

Local Representative:
200 Maryland Avenue, N.E.
Suite 301
Washington, D.C. 20242
202/963-4655

Institute of Puerto Rican Culture (Instituto de Cultura Puertorriquena)
Apartado Postal 4184
San Juan, Puerto Rico 09005
809/723-2115

Virgin Islands Council on the Arts
Caravelle Arcade
Christiansted
St. Croix, U.S.V.I. 00820
809/773-3075, Ext. 3

Canada
Provincial Arts Councils

Alberta
Department of Culture, Youth
and Recreation
Government of Alberta
11th Floor, CN Tower
10004 104th Avenue
Edmonton, Alberta T5J OK5

British Columbia
First Citizens' Fund
Parliament Buildings
Victoria, B.C.

Manitoba
201-185 Carlton Street
Winnipeg, Manitoba R3C 1P3
204/943-6325

New Brunswick
"The Playhouse"
Fredericton, New Brunswick

Newfoundland (Cultural Affairs)
Newfoundland Arts and Culture
Centre
P.O. Box 1854
St. John's, Newfoundland

Nova Scotia-Cultural Resources Program
1747 Summer Street
Halifax, Nova Scotia

Ontario-Arts Council
151 Bloor Street West, 5th Floor
Ministry of Colleges and
Universities
Toronto, Ontario, M5S IT6
461/961-1660

Prince Edward Island (Department of the Environment and Tourism)
P.O. Box 2000
Charlottetown, Prince Edward
Island

Quebec (Ministere des Affaires Culturelles)
Hotel de Gouvernement
Quebec 4, Quebec

Saskatchewan Arts Board
200 Lakeshore Drive
Regina, Saskatchewan S4S OA4

Yukon
Department of Education
Recreation Branch
P.O. Box 2703
Whitehorse, Y.T.

State Humanities Agencies

Alabama
Office of the Dean of Humanities
and Behavioral Science
University of Alabama
Huntsville, Alabama

Alaska Humanities Forum
429 D Street, Room 211
Loussac Sogn Building
Anchorage, Alaska 99501

Arizona Council on the Humanities and Public Policy
Post Office Box 3183
Tempe, Arizona 85283

Arkansas Humanities Program
University of Arkansas
Little Rock, Arkansas 72201

California Council on the Humanities in Public Policy
University of San Francisco
San Francisco, California 94117

Colorado Humanities Program
855 Broadway
Boulder, Colorado 80302

Connecticut Humanities Council
250 Court Street
Middletown, Connecticut 06457

Delaware Humanities Council
2600 Pennsylvania Avenue
Wilmington, Delaware 19806

Florida Citizens' Committee for the Humanities
Post Office Box 12657
University Station
Gainesville, Florida 32604

Georgia Committee for the Humanities
Georgia Center for Continuing
Education
Athens, Georgia 30601

Hawaii Committee for the Humanities
465 S. King Street
Honolulu, Hawaii 96813

Idaho Association for the Humanities
Post Office Box 424
Boise, Idaho 83701

Illinois Council for Humanities and Public Policy
411 Gregory Hall
University of Illinois
Urbana, Illinois 61801

Indiana Committee for the Humanities
4200 Northwestern Avenue
Indianapolis, Indiana 46205

Iowa Board for Public Programs in the Humanities
c/o Division of Extension
C-207 East Hall
University of Iowa
Iowa City, Iowa 52240

Kansas Committee for the Humanities
1018 Merchants Bank Building
8th and Jackson Streets
Topeka, Kansas 66612

Kentucky Humanities Council, Inc.
206 Breckinridge Hall
University of Kentucky
Lexington, Kentucky 40506

Louisiana Committee for the Humanities
Box 12, Loyola University
New Orleans, Louisiana 70118

Maine Humanities Council
5 Highland Avenue
Camden, Maine 04843

Maryland Committee for the Humanities and Public Policy
Room 307, Maryland Hall
The Johns Hopkins University
34th and Charles Streets
Baltimore, Maryland 21218

Massachusetts Committee for the Humanities
Amherst, Massachusetts 01002

Michigan Committee for the Humanities
Department of Continuing Education
Room 7, Kellogg Center
Michigan State University
East Lansing, Michigan 48824

Minnesota Humanities Commission
Metro Square
St. Paul, Minnesota 55108

Mississippi Committee for the Humanities
Post Office Box 335
University, Mississippi 38677

Missouri State Committee for the Humanities
Box 1145A, Washington University
St. Louis, Missouri 63130

Montana Committee for the Humanities
University of Montana
Missoula, Montana 59801

Nebraska Committee for the Humanities
RFD 2, Box 65A
Kearney, Nebraska 68847

Nevada Humanities Committee
1101 North Virginia Street
Reno, Nevada 89503

New Hampshire Council for the Humanities
Box 271
Meriden, New Hampshire 03770

New Jersey Committee on the Humanities
Rutgers University
137 Church Street
New Brunswick, New Jersey 08903

New Mexico Humanities Council
300 Scholes Hall
The University of New Mexico
Albuquerque, New Mexico 87131

North Carolina Committee for the Humanities
1209 West Market Street
Greensboro, North Carolina 27403

North Dakota Committee for the Humanities
Box 136
Dickinson State College
Dickinson, North Dakota 58601

The Ohio Committee for Public Programs in the Humanities
2199 East Main Street
Columbus, Ohio 43209

Oklahoma Humanities Committee
11018 Quail Creek Road
Oklahoma City, Oklahoma 73120

Oregon Committee for the Humanities
1633 S.W. Park
Portland, Oregon 97201

Pennsylvania
The Public Committee for the Humanities
Bucknell University
Lewisburg, Pennsylvania 17837

Rhode Island Committee for the Humanities
86 Weybosset, Room 807
Providence, Rhode Island 02903

South Carolina Committee for the Humanities
Columbia Building, Suite 604
Columbia, South Carolina 29201

South Dakota Committee for the Humanities
Box 35, University Station
Brookings, South Dakota 57006

Tennessee Committee for Relating the Humanities to the Public Policy
Suite 369, Provident Building
Chattanooga, Tennessee 37402

Texas Committee for the Humanities and Public Policy
P.O. Box 19096
University of Texas at Arlington
Arlington, Texas 76019

Utah Endowment for the Humanities and Public Policy
316 Carlson Hall
University of Utah
Salt Lake City, Utah 84112

Vermont Committee for the Humanities
Grant House
P.O Box 58
Hyde Park, Vermont 05655

Virginia Foundation for the Humanities Public Policy
205 Miller Hall
University of Virginia
Charlottesville, Virginia 22903

Appendix B

Washington Commission for the Humanities
Room 3229, Library
Evergreen State College
Olympia, Washington 98505

West Virginia Committee for the Humanities
Department of English
West Virginia University
Morgantown, West Virginia 26506

Wisconsin Humanities Committee
c/o State Historical Society of Wisconsin
816 State Street
Madison, Wisconsin 53706

Wyoming Council for the Humanities
Box 3274, University Station
Laramie, Wyoming 82071

Appendix C

Foundation Information

The Foundation Center sponsors regional depositories of current information. All of these libraries are open to the public.

Graduate Social Science Library
Stephens Hall
University of California
Berkeley, California 94720

Foundation Collection
Reference Department
University Research Library
University of California
Los Angeles, California 90024

Foundation Library Collection
Atlanta Public Library
126 Carnegie Way, N.W.
Atlanta, Georgia 30303

The Newberry Library
60 West Walton Street
Chicago, Illinois 60610

Associated Foundation of
Greater Boston
One Boston Place
Boston, Massachusetts 02109

The Danforth Foundation
222 South Central Avenue
St. Louis, Missouri 63105

Cleveland Foundation Library
700 National City Bank Building
Cleveland, Ohio 44114

Regional Foundation Library
The Hogg Foundation for Mental
Health
The University of Texas
Austin, Texas 78712

Appendix D

Regional Branches of the National Archives

The National Archives, Washington, D.C. 20408, document American history from the First Continental Congress and include the permanently valuable records of the three branches of the Federal Government.

The eleven regional archives branches preserve and make available for research use those U.S. Government records of permanent value created and maintained by field offices of Federal agencies that are useful primarily for documenting regional and local activities.

Records common to the branch offices include records of District Courts of the United States, records of the United States Courts of Appeals, records of the Bureau of Indian Affairs, records of the Bureau of Customs, records of the Office of the Chief of Engineers, and others, including Bureau of Land Management and National Park Service, Forest Service, and many others.

Boston
(Serves Connecticut, Maine, Massachusetts, New Hampshire, Rhode Island, and Vermont.)
380 Trapelo Road
Waltham, Massachusetts 02154

New York
(Serves New Jersey, New York, Puerto Rico, and the Virgin Islands)
Building 22—MOT Bayonne
Bayonne, New Jersey 07002

Philadelphia
(Serves Delaware and Pennsylvania; for the loan of microfilm also serves the District of Columbia, Maryland, Virginia and West Virginia.)
5000 Wissahickon Avenue
Philadelphia, Pennsylvania 19144

Atlanta
(Serves Alabama, Georgia, Florida, Kentucky, Mississippi, North Carolina, South Carolina, and Tennessee.)
1557 St. Joseph Avenue
East Point, Georgia 30344

Chicago

(Serves Illinois, Indiana,
Michigan, Minnesota, Ohio, and
Wisconsin.)
5358 South Pulaski Road
Chicago, Illinois 60629

Kansas City

(Serves Iowa, Kansas, Missouri,
and Nebraska.)
2306 East Bannister Road
Kansas City, Missouri 64131

Forth Worth

(Serves Arkansas, Louisiana,
New Mexico, Oklahoma, and
Texas.)
4900 Hemphill Street (building
address)
P.O. Box 6216 (mailing address)
Fort Worth, Texas 76115

Denver

(Serves Colorado, Montana,
North Dakota, South Dakota,
Utah, and Wyoming.)
Building 48, Denver Federal
Center
Denver, Colorado 80225

San Francisco

(Serves California except
southern California, Hawaii,
Nevada except Clark County,
and the Pacific Ocean area.)
1000 Commodore Drive
San Bruno, California 94066

Los Angeles

(Serves Arizona; the southern
California counties of Imperial,
Inyo, Kern, Los Angeles,
Orange, Riverside, San
Bernardino, San Diego, San Luis
Obispo, Santa Barbara, and
Ventura; and Clark County,
Nevada.)
24000 Avila Road
Lagune Niguel, California 90377

Seattle

(Serves Alaska, Idaho, Oregon,
and Washington.)
6125 Sand Point Way, N.E.
Seattle, Washington 98115

Appendix E

Criteria for Evaluation for the National Register

The following statement is taken from the leaflet of the National Register of Historic Places. The leaflet is available from the National Park Service, USDI, Washington, D.C.

The following criteria are designed to guide the States, Federal agencies, and the Secretary of the Interior in evaluating potential entries (other than areas of the National Park System and national historic landmarks) for the National Register:

The quality of significance in American history, architecture, archeology, and culture is present in districts, sites, buildings, structures, and objects that possess integrity of location, design, setting, materials, workmanship, feeling, and association, and:

A. that are associated with events that have made a significant contribution to the broad patterns of our history; or

B. that are associated with the lives of persons significant in our past; or

C. that embody the distinctive characteristics of a type, period, or method of construction, or that represent the work of a master, or that possess high artistic values, or that represent a significant and distinguishable entity whose components may lack individual distinction; or

D. that have yielded, or may be likely to yield, information important in prehistory or history.

Ordinarily, cemeteries, birthplaces, or graves of historical figures, properties owned by religious institutions or used for religious pruposes, structures that have been moved from their original locations, reconstructed historic buildings, properties primarily commemorative in nature, and properties that have achieved significance within the past 50 years shall not be considered eligible for the National Register. However, such properties will qualify if they are integral parts of districts that do meet the criteria or if they fall within the following categories:

A. a religious property deriving primary significance from architectural or artistic distinction or historical importance; or

B. a building or structure removed from its original location but which is significant primarily for architectural value, or which is the surviving structure most importantly associated with a historic person or event; or

C. a birthplace or grave of a historical figure of outstanding importance if there is no other appropriate site or building directly associated with his productive life; or

D. a cemetery which derives its primary significance from graves of persons of transcendent importance, from age, from distinctive design features, or from association with historic events; or

E. a reconstructed building when accurately executed in a suitable environment and presented in a dignified manner as part of a restoration master plan, and when no other building or structure with the same association has survived; or

F. a property primarily commemorative in intent if design, age, tradition, or symbolic value has invested it with its own historical significance; or

G. a property achieving significance within the past 50 years if it is of exceptional importance.

State Historic Preservation Officers

Following is a list of officials primarily responsible for National Historic Preservation Act programs in each state:

Alabama: Director, Alabama Dept. of Archives & History, Chairman, Alabama Historical Commission, Archives & History Building, Montgomery, AL 36104.

Alaska: Director, Division of Parks, 323 E. 4th Ave., Anchorage, AK 99501.

Arizona: Director, State Parks Board, 1688 W. Adams, Phoenix, AZ 85007.

Arkansas: Director, Arkansas Dept. of Parks and Tourism, State Capitol, Rm. 149, Little Rock, AR 72201.

California: Director, Dept. of Parks & Recreation, State Resources Agency, Box 2390, Sacramento, CA 95811.

Colorado: Chairman, State Historical Society, Colorado State Museum, 200 14th Ave., Denver, CO 80203.

Connecticut: Director, Connecticut Historical Commission, 59 S. Prospect St., Hartford, CT 06106.

Delaware: Secretary of State of Delaware, Acting Director, Division of Historical & Cultural Affairs, Hall of Records, Dover, DE 19901.

Florida: Director, Division of Archives, History & Records Management, Dept. of State, 401 E. Gaines St., Tallahassee, FL 32304.

Georgia: Chief, Historic Preservation Section, Dept. of Natural Resources, 710 Trinity-Washington Building, 270 Washington St., SW, Atlanta, GA 30334.

Hawaii: Chairman, Dept. of Land and Natural Resources, Box 621, Honolulu, HI 96809

Idaho: Director, Idaho Historical Society, 610 N. Julia Davis Drive, Boise, ID 83706.

Illinois: Director, Dept. of Conservation, 602 State Office Building, 400 S. Spring St., Springfield, IL 62706.

Indiana: Director, Dept. of Natural Resources, 608 State Office Building, Indianapolis, IN 46204

Iowa: Director, State Historical Dept., B-13 MacLean Hall, Iowa City, IA 52242.

Kansas: Executive Director, Kansas State Historical Society, 120 W. 10th St., Topeka, KS 66612.

Kentucky: Director, Kentucky Heritage Commission, 401 Wapping St., Frankfort, KY 40601

Louisiana: Director, Dept. of Art, Historical & Cultural Preservation, Old State Capitol, Baton Rouge, LA 70801.

Maine: Director, Maine Historical Preservation Commission, 31 Western Ave., Augusta, ME 04330.

Maryland: Director, Maryland Historical Trust, 2525 Riva Rd., Annapolis, MD 21401.

Massachusetts: Executive Director, Massachusetts Historical Commission, 40 Beacon St., Boston, MA 02108.

Michigan: Director, Michigan History Division, Dept. of State, Lansing, MI 48918.

Minnesota: Director, Minnesota Historical Society, 690 Cedar St., St. Paul, MN 55101.

Mississippi: Director, State of Mississippi Dept. of Archives and History, Box 571, Jackson, MS 39205.

Missouri: Director, Missouri State Park Board, Box 176, 1204 Jefferson Building, Jefferson City, MO 65101.

Montana: Administrator, Recreation and Parks Division, Dept. of Fish and Game, Mitchell Building, Helena, MT 59601.

Nebraska: Director, Nebraska State Historical Society, 1500 R St., Lincoln, NB 68508.

Nevada: Administrator, Division of State Parks, 201 S. Fall St., Carson City, NV 89701.

New Hampshire: Commissioner, Dept. of Resources and Economic Development, Box 856, Concord, NH 03301.

New Jersey: Commissioner, Dept. of Environmental Protection, Box 1420, Trenton, NJ 08625

New Mexico: State Planning Officer, State Capitol, 403 Capitol Building, Santa Fe, NM 87501.

New York: Commissioner, Parks and Recreation, Rm. 303, S. Swan St. Bldg., Albany, NY 12223.

North Carolina: Director, Division of Archives & History, Dept. of Cultural Resources, 109 E. Jones St., Raleigh, NC 27611.

North Dakota: Superintendent, State Historical Society of North Dakota, Liberty Memorial Building, Bismark, ND 58501.

Ohio: Acting Director, Ohio Historical Society, Interstate #71, at 17th Ave., Columbus, OH 43211.

Oklahoma: George Shirk, 1108 Colcord Bldg., Oklahoma City, OK 73102.

Oregon: State Parks Superintendent, 300 State Highway Building, Salem, OR 97310.

Pennsylvania: Executive Director, Pennsylvania Historical and Museum Commission, Box 1026, Harrisburg, PA 17120.

Rhode Island: Director, Rhode Island Dept. of Community Affairs, 150 Washington St., Providence, RI 02903.

South Carolina: Director, State Archives Department, 1430 Senate St., Columbia, SC 29211.

South Dakota: Director, Office of Cultural Preservation, Dept. of Education & Cultural Affairs, State Capitol, Pierre, SD 57501.

Tennessee: Executive Director, Tennessee Historical Commission, 170 2nd Ave. North, Suite 100, Nashville, TN 37219.

Texas: Executive Director, Texas State Historical Survey Committee, Box 12276, Capitol Station, Austin, TX 78711.

Utah: Director, Division of State History, .603 E. South Temple, Salt Lake City, UT 84102.

Vermont: Director, Vermont Division of Historic Sites, Pavilion Building, Montpelier, VT 05602.

Virginia: Executive Director, Virginia Historic Landmarks Commission, 221 Governor St., Richmond, VA 23219.

Washington: Director, Washington State Parks & Recreation Commission, Box 1128, Olympia, WA 98504.

West Virginia: West Virginia Antiquities Commission, Old Mountainlair, West Virginia University, Morgantown, WV 26506.

Wisconsin: Director, State Historical Society of Wisconsin, 816 State St., Madison, WI 53706.

Wyoming: Director, Wyoming Recreation Commission, 604 East 25th St., Box 309, Cheyenne, WY 82001.

D.C.: Acting Director, Office of Housing & Community Development, Rm. 112A, District Building, 14th and E St., NW., Washington, DC 20004.

American Samoa: Territorial Historic Preservation Officer, Dept. of Public Works, Government of American Samoa 96799.

Puerto Rico: Institute of Puerto Rico Culture, Apartado 4184, San Juan, PR 00905.

Guam: Director, Dept. of Commerce, Government of Guam, Box 682, Agana, GU 96910.

Trust Territory: Chief, Land Resources Branch, Dept. of Resources and Development, Trust Territory of the Pacific Islands, Saipan, Marianas Islands 96950.

Virgin Islands: Planning Director, Virgin Islands Planning Board, Charlotte Amalie, St. Thomas, VI 00801.

National Trust for Historic Preservation: President, National Trust for Historic Preservation, 740 Jackson Place, N.W., Washington, DC 20006.

Index